MW01232297

Compel Them To Come In

Reaching People with Disabilities through the Local Church

Presented By
Special Touch Ministry, Inc.

Compiled and Edited by
Tom Leach

authorHOUSE®

AuthorHouse™
1663 Liberty Drive
Bloomington, IN 47403
www.authorhouse.com
Phone: 1-800-839-8640

First published by AuthorHouse 2/3/2010

ISBN: 978-1-4490-7586-6 (sc)

Library of Congress Control Number: 2010900635

Printed in the United States of America
Bloomington, Indiana

This book is printed on acid-free paper.

Table of Contents

Credits

Editor and Lead Writer
Tom Leach

Copy Editor
Karen Braithwaite

Executive Editorial Consultant
Charlie Chivers

Project Manager
Debbie Chivers

Cover Design
Trace Chiodo

Proofreader
Robin Smith

Creative Consultant
Gayle Leach

Contributing Writers
(In Alphabetical Order)
Larry Campbell
Charlie Chivers
Gayle Leach
Sarah Sykes
Paul Weingartner

Special Thanks to:
Ruth Dusing
Peter and Beverly Scheuermann

To all of the members of the
Special Touch Ministry family
who have
"picked up the towel"
and washed feet
with the hands and the heart of Jesus
since 1982

and

To each member of
our ministry family
who has gone ahead of us to wait with Him.

A Word from the Founder and President of Special Touch Ministry, Inc.

Close your eyes for a moment and imagine being born into permanent darkness. Continue the journey. Your eyes see but your ears don't hear. You are born into a sub-culture that largely rejects both the label of disability and the remedies for your condition.

In this next vignette you are traveling to meet your fiancée when in the space of ninety seconds while adjusting for an oncoming truck, you roll your car over three times down an embankment. After regaining consciousness you find that you are paralyzed from the chest down. In the instant it took for your vertebrae to puncture the spinal cord, you have been suddenly and violently transformed into a stranger you do not know.

Imagine again that you leave home on your motorcycle for a five minute trip to the market. You are broadsided by a car whose driver ran a stop sign. When you awaken, not only will you use a wheelchair the rest of your life, a head injury has robbed you of your ability to speak or form language. From now on you will think thoughts like always, experience emotions like always, but your wife and kids will never again hear your voice. For the rest of your life you will speak to them and the world only with your eyes.

As we near the end of this trip through "time, space and mind" you find your adult body has the mind of a child. Your thoughts are of the simplest kind and the rest of your mind is adrift in a confused fog. Finally, life finds you becoming a parent. Imagine one of these two situations. Either you are sitting in a hospital in the last scenario, waiting word on your wife and child and a grim faced doctor appears with a diagnosis of Down's Syndrome or at one in the morning your phone rings startling you awake, the messenger on the other end of the phone tells you that your child has been in a life changing accident.

These people and tens of thousands more like them have been the constituents of Special Touch Ministry since 1982. They represent the 20% of the American population who live with disabilities. Eighty percent of this people group does not attend church. Perhaps you yourself will never be personally touched by disability and your life never ravaged by its ramifications, but consider for a moment the exercise you just went on. As you passed through each vignette were you touched at all by the pain, grief, anger, fear, isolation and hopelessness that the Goliath called disability brings into the families it touches? Does it stir the compassion of Christ within you and call you to action? If your answer to these questions is yes, you are not alone. The Lord is drafting legions of workers in these final moments of redemptive history to reach this neglected mission field with the blessed Good News of Jesus Christ. Answering this call can be a scary thing. You may be frightened by people who on the outset may seem so different. Rest assured that as you take this journey you will find many lifelong friends who have much more in common with you than you ever imagined. They smile, they laugh, they love, and they cry when they are hurt. Most importantly, each one has a soul that like you and me needs to be infused with the life and love of Jesus Christ.

You may feel unprepared and ill-equipped to pursue the call and tempted to quit before you start. This book, written by people with decades of experience in evangelizing people with disabilities of all kinds, will give you the confidence and courage to plunge into the greatest adventure in love and servanthood you have ever known.

May God bless you richly as you reach people with disabilities in your community and in your world!

Charlie Chivers

Foreword

This handbook has been written specifically to help the local church bring the gospel to people in their community who has been impacted by intellectual and physical disabilities. It is built on two of Christ's admonitions. The first is His call in Luke, chapter 14, to the Church to bring in and embrace the disenfranchised, including those with disabilities. The second is His call in John, chapter 13, to individual Christians to "wash feet."

"Washing feet" is probably the best biblical analogy, illustration, and demonstration of evangelizing and serving the concerns of people with disabilities. In biblical times people who were disenfranchised or had disabilities of many kinds probably went unwashed because they were unable to do it themselves or find someone who was willing to humble themselves to serve those whom society had discarded.

The biggest misconception encountered by those who have the task of recruiting other Christians into working in this mission field is the idea that it takes someone *special* to work with people with disabilities. One of the most powerful aspects in Jesus' demonstration of washing feet was the very fact that it *did not require someone with any special qualifications*. Any Christian can wash feet. All that is required are willing hands and a compassionate heart.

"Washing feet" has become emblematic of the philosophy of Special Touch Ministry. We have adopted this simple demonstration by Jesus because in its simplicity it is profoundly powerful. Washing the feet of others is to enter into their humiliation. It identifies with their weaknesses and limitations without stripping them of their dignity. It ministers to the necessities those weaknesses create while removing barriers to fellowship and understanding. It involves coming down without putting down. Songwriter Michael Card referred to it as, "the will of water and the tenderness of the towel" to cleanse, refresh, renew, and restore.

Willingly coming down and entering into the humiliation of another person while ministering to their necessities is a powerful demonstration of the love and reality of God. Washing their feet helps open broken hearts and enables wounded spirits to become receptive to the gospel's message. However, washing feet can be very intimidating even for those who are compassionate and willing. This book has been written in order to help people who are willing to pick up the towel but would like some advice on how to use that towel most effectively. The contributors to this book have all worked in ministry to people with disabilities for many years. Some of them have disabilities of their own that they must contend with every day. All of them desire to make their life experience available to you through this book.

This is intended to be a nuts and bolts how-to book. It emphasizes practical ways for you to become friends and share Christ with people impacted by physical and mental disability and begin an outreach to them through your church. This text is designed to be a "disability ministry conference" between two covers. In fact, each chapter can be taught as an individual workshop. Because of this feature, some material is repeated but applied in a different way or viewed from different perspectives applicable to the subject discussed in that chapter.

One thing this book is definitely not intended to do is answer all of the biblical questions regarding disability issues. This book is intentionally *not* scripture intensive. For an in-depth study of what the Bible has to say about disability issues, we recommend our brief companion publication *When You Give a Feast*.

A Word about the Language of Disability

A major topic in this handbook is the language used to refer to people with disabilities. While no one wishes to be offensive, and Christians need to be culturally sensitive—if not politically correct, the ongoing evolution of terminology can be a problem for someone in disability ministry. First of all, it is very difficult to stay abreast with what is currently considered correct. Secondly, it is becoming increasingly more difficult to determine what exactly these new terms mean. The continuing trend is toward terms that are vague and non-specific. While this may achieve the goals of political correctness, it does not help a non-professional accurately define conditions and parameters related to disability.

The problem with the currently popular term *moderate intellectual disability* is that it can often leave the mistaken impression that a person with that condition is not as impaired as someone who is *low functioning* or *mentally retarded*. Actually, there is no distinction between them; they are three different labels for the same condition. Unfortunately, words that may sound harsh, such as "low functioning," sometimes give a more accurate word picture of the condition or impairment of an individual or people group under discussion.

Although every effort has been made to use terminology that is compassionate, current, and culturally sensitive, sometimes for the purposes of accuracy or clarity, terms that are not currently in vogue are used. *These terms are always used to describe a condition or impairment and are in no way intended to be construed as a value judgment on an individual or people group.* Likewise, in the interest of readability, "disability ministry" is sometimes used instead of the phrase "ministry to people with disabilities."

A Word about Disability Statistics

Some statistics generated by disability information sources are unreliable because disability definitions are not standardized. There is not even agreement on what constitutes disability. The most consistent and reliable figures are those produced by the Census Bureau and the National Organization on Disability which place the number at about 58 million. Many people are often hungry for the very latest numbers. The most recent and reliable numbers are still from the 2000 census. However even the census does not count people with disabilities who are under five years of age or over sixty-five. For statistical updates check the following sources:

The United States Census Bureau
The United States Department of Labor
The National Organization on Disability
The Multiple Sclerosis Web Site

A Word about the Culture of the Deaf

This book does not deal in depth with ministry to the deaf because as a culture they do not want to be identified, defined, or labeled as having a disability. They believe that their condition creates a culture from which they relate to the world. We respect that position but recommend that churches provide sign language interpreters and amplification devices in their services.

Introduction

THE FOUNDATION OF DISABILITY MINISTRY: JESUS CHRIST

The purpose of this introduction is to provide people called to disability ministry with the biblical foundation for what they already feel in their heart and a resource they can use in communicating that call to others. Both the founder and central focus of ministry to people with disabilities is our Lord, Jesus Christ.

WE HAVE A MISSION

The essential purpose of Christ and the Church has always been a search and rescue mission. Jesus came to "seek and to save" the lost. Churches are lighthouses for the lost and hospitals for the hurting. The Great Commission is the ultimate and highest example of Christian inclusion. It is a call and a command to reach *every* individual with the good news that Jesus Christ died for the sins of the world:

> *And He said to them, 'Go into all the world and preach the gospel to all creation.'* (Mark 16:15 New American Standard Bible).

Disability enters into that mission because disabling conditions are pervasive the world over. Disability can be defined as any physical or mental impairment that inhibits one or more major life activities or functions. The most recent statistics available (the 2000 US census) states that one in five people in the United States live with a physical or cognitive disability. Virtually every family will be impacted in some way. Therefore, disability ministry should not be part of what we do; it should be at the heart of what we do. In giving the Great Commission to the church, Christ saw a world that was dying before His eyes. He recognized that salvation is the greatest need in every segment of society. *Disability ministry defined is responding to that commission with a commitment to evangelize, disciple, and equip people with disabilities to use their gifts to build up the body of Christ.* The scope of this encompasses the entire disability community. It includes people with disabilities, their families and other care providers.

WE HAVE A MANDATE

By example and by command, Jesus Christ mandated disability ministry. First of all, people with disabilities were at the dynamic center of Christ's earthly ministry. They were right where His power was being poured out. Matthew tells us:

> *Then His fame went throughout all Syria; and they brought to Him all sick people who were afflicted with various diseases and torment. . . epileptics and paralytics, and He healed them.* (4:24)

> *The blind see and the lame walk, . . . and the deaf hear;. . .* (11:5)

> *Then great multitudes came to Him, having with them the lame, blind, mute, maimed, and many others; and they laid them down at Jesus' feet, and He healed them.* (15:30)

Secondly, the evangelism of those who are disenfranchised, including people with disabilities, is a heaven or hell issue for the Church.

> *Then He will also say to those on the left hand, "Depart from me, you cursed, into the everlasting fire prepared for the devil and his angels: . . ." Then He will answer them, saying, "Assuredly, I say to you, inasmuch as you did not do it to one of the least of these, you did not do it to Me."* (Matt. 25:41, 45)

If salvation is not of works, how can Jesus make works, any works, even reaching out to the least of these, a condition on which salvation rests? The answer is that reaching out to "the least of these" is a tell-tale mark of a born-again heart, a heart that beats as one with the Father, and like the Father, is "not willing that any should perish" (2 Pet. 3:9).

Thirdly, the Church is to make a special effort to bring people with disabilities into their midst and to treat them as honored guests. This is borne out by Christ's instructions in Luke, chapter 14:

When you give a dinner or a supper, do not ask your friends, your brothers, your relatives, nor rich neighbors, lest they also invite you back, and you be repaid. But when you give a feast, invite the poor, the maimed, the lame, the blind. And you will be blessed, because they cannot repay you; for you shall be repaid at the resurrection of the just (12-14).

Then the master of the house, being angry, said to His servant, "Go out quickly into the streets and lanes of the city, and bring in here the poor and the maimed and the lame and the blind.". . . Then the master said to the servant, "Go out into the highways and hedges, and compel them to come in, that my house may be filled" (21, 23).

WE HAVE A MODEL

People with disabilities live in a raw, harsh reality. They are painfully aware that their conditions and circumstances are often ugly and distasteful to others, and that their lifestyle and behaviors are sometimes interpreted as being weird, abnormal, and bizarre. As a result, they are also painfully aware that the people around them are often uncomfortable or revolted. Christ's example of humility, empathy, and servanthood teaches us that the compassion of the Body must be greater than its need for comfort. Jesus took the ugly, dirt-encrusted feet of his disciples in His holy hands and washed them. People with disabilities are changed by the gospel when they are confronted by a Christian who embodies and demonstrates the love of Jesus by serving. The best model or analogy the Bible has for reaching out and touching the lives of people with disabilities is washing feet.

You call me Teacher and Lord, and you say well, for so I am. If I then, your Lord and Teacher, have washed your feet, you also ought to wash one another's feet. For I have given you an example, that you should do as I have done to you. Most assuredly, I say to you, a servant is not greater than his master, nor is he who is sent greater than he who sent him. If you know these things, blessed are you if you do them (John 13:13-17).

WE HAVE A METHOD

The task before us can seem overwhelming, but in Luke 14:21-23, Jesus gives us a way to approach the problem. We believe that if this evangelism approach is followed aggressively, compassionately, and prayerfully, it can be successfully adapted by any church. The method can be summarized as follows:

- ☐ Go out beyond your walls.
- ☐ Seek out those who are disenfranchised.
- ☐ Canvass your community.
- ☐ Meet felt needs.
- ☐ Compel them to come in.
- ☐ Do it now.

This book is designed to help you successfully use this method in your church. Hopefully, it will give you the basics you will need to give birth to a ministry that will bless your congregation, your community, and your world.

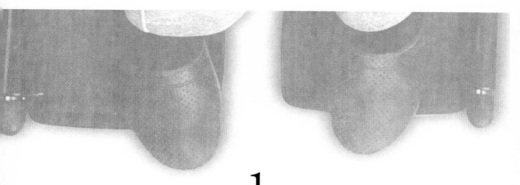

1.

"Preparing the Banquet"

OBJECTIVES

- ☐ To create awareness of the need for disability evangelism and ministry in your community
- ☐ To be able to capitalize on commitments to servanthood
- ☐ To create an atmosphere of love and acceptance for people with disabilities in your church
- ☐ To explain the need for accessible facilities
- ☐ To fit into the flow of administration and ministry within the church

THE CONCEPT:

When the body of Christ comes together and gathers in His name, it is a celebration—in effect, a banquet—where acceptance, fellowship, worship, and ministry are available to all. The church "prepares the banquet" by readying their hearts, ministries, and facilities for heavenly service.

Foundation Scripture

Luke 14:12-14: The Parable of the Great Feast

The Definition of "Disability Ministry":

Disability ministry or ministry to people with disabilities is responding to Christ's Great Commission with a commitment to evangelize, disciple, and equip people impacted by disability to use their ministry gifts to build up and complete the body of Christ. The scope of this ministry includes those with physical and intellectual disabilities, their families and caregivers.

CREATING AWARENESS:

Accept the Call

God calls His people into ministry in many ways. Rev. Tommy Barnett pastors a large, thriving church in Phoenix, Arizona. Over the years he has developed a proven method for starting new outreaches to the community. From time to time, a member of the congregation will come in and propose a new ministry. Pastor Barnett listens to them share their burden, and then challenges them to act on that burden by taking the lead in getting the ministry started. If you have a burden for seeing people with disabilities come to know Christ, it is probably an indication that God wants to use *you*. There is an old proverb that says, "If not us, then who? If not now, then when? If not here, then where?" That saying becomes an imperative that compels us to act when we consider the admonitions of Jesus: *"As long as it is day, we must do the work of Him who sent me. Night is coming, when no one can work"* (John 9:4 New International Version).

Compassion goes beyond weeping because someone is in a wheelchair or has a severe mental disability; compassion is the love of God within us driving us to serve someone in need.

Get Involved Personally

Act on the burden God has given you. Don't be afraid of starting alone and starting small. When asked how to begin a music ministry, Bill Gaither said, "The best way to get started is to get started." The same is true of disability ministry. Here are some simple ways you can begin letting the Lord use you in reaching people with disabilities:

- ☐ Bring a neighbor with a disability to church.
- ☐ Bring Christian music, videos, and literature to shut-ins with disabilities.
- ☐ Visit nursing homes and community-based residential facilities (CBRF). Many are looking for people who will come in and share on a consistent basis.
- ☐ Meet the felt needs of a neighbor with a disability: do yard work, laundry, grocery shopping, etc.
- ☐ Volunteer as a Special Touch caregiver at a Summer Get Away or volunteer for another disability ministry such as becoming a reader for the National Center for the Blind.

Diving in and getting personally involved gives one experience and a testimony of God's faithfulness. God can use that testimony to draw other workers into partnership with you.

Pray to the Lord of the Harvest

Prayer is the foundation for success in any ministry endeavor. Prayer is our admission that we need more in our ministry than the latest winning strategies from the last conference we attended or the last teaching to which we listened. Pouring our hearts out to the Master demonstrates our reliance on Him to provide His power, His plan, and His people for the completion of the task He has given us.

As you continue in disability ministry, share with others about what you are doing. Ask them to pray for you. Over time, you will develop a network of intercessors that will undergird your ministry in prayer.

Cast Vision

Casting vision is planting what God has placed in your heart into the hearts of others. You do it by placing the need before them, showing or reminding them of a Biblical response, and demonstrating how they can be a blessing. You cast your vision by doing the following:

Stand on the Scriptural Foundation

We thought it appropriate to introduce this guide by identifying the scriptural foundation for disability ministry. That foundation is Jesus Himself. Use this material as a tool in communicating your vision, but try not to use it as a Scriptural sledgehammer.

Involve your Pastor

For both spiritual and pragmatic reasons, it is imperative that you involve your pastor. From a spiritual point of view, every ministry needs a covering to nurture it, encourage it, and provide accountability for it. Your pastor can also give you vital prayer support and insights on servanthood and personal interaction. From a pragmatic standpoint, he is the key to the pulpit, and the pulpit is the key to the congregation. He is also the key to the church board, which is the key to most of the church's resources. When sharing your ministry burden with *anyone*, be prayerful, tactful, and respectful. When presenting the need to your pastor, be willing to be part of the solution.

Use Available Resources

Here are some more weapons you can use in your awareness arsenal:

- Ask your pastor if he would prayerfully consider preaching and teaching on the need for disability ministry, the biblical view of disability, and servanthood.
- Talk to your C.E. Director about offering an elective Sunday school or mid-week class on disability awareness and effective ways of evangelizing people with disabilities.

□ Put together an information sheet of disability statistics and facts for use by the pastor and board, and by the congregation on Disability Awareness Sunday. Try to tailor it to the needs of your community and congregation. Much information is available at your public library or on the Internet. Always note that statistics vary, and give only a general indication of the need.

□ Plan a Disability Awareness Sunday or ministry-training seminar. Special Touch Ministry can assist you in these areas.

□ Get together and share your burden with those who are already impacted by a disability in some way. Don't forget to include those who have a spouse or a child with a disability.

□ Utilize Special Touch events to expose people with and without disabilities to disability ministry. Use them as opportunities to be encouraged by others who are involved in disability ministry.

CAPITALIZING ON COMMITMENTS TO SERVANTHOOD:

Establish a Core Group

Disability Awareness presentations usually help congregations build a fresh emotional link to people with disabilities and their needs. God's call to their hearts for involvement must be solidified before their tears dry and are forgotten. After your Disability Awareness Sunday, you need to recruit your core group. They will be the heart of your disability ministry team. They will help you carry the ball. *The core group is the most important element of an effective and lasting ministry. Recruit people who will be there when the tough times come.* The core group is the engine on the disability ministry train. Prayer and passion are the fuel. Parents of children with disabilities and those with spouses who have a disability many times make great core group members because they already have the passion for it.

Make a Plan: Everyone Can Do Something

Next, map out a strategy for ministry to the community, or if you are in a large city, draw a circle with a ten-mile radius around the church. Strategies for community evangelism are covered in the next chapter, but here is an example of an effective disability ministry.

"The Beaver Dam Strategy"

Special Touch in Beaver Dam, Wisconsin is a thriving chapter in the network of Special Touch support groups. They use a comprehensive and balanced approach for affecting those in their sphere of influence. Their plan provides room in their schedule for:

- ☐ Monthly meetings for fellowship and support
- ☐ Bi-weekly mothers' coffee fellowships for evangelism and caregiver support
- ☐ Periodic appearances at community events to increase exposure and provoke involvement
- ☐ Periodic fundraisers to meet expenses and support missionaries to people with disabilities

The group in Beaver Dam identified four areas of need: fellowship and support, evangelism, community involvement, and ministry support and expansion. Then they designed events and a workable schedule to help meet those needs.

Disability Ministry Programs for the Local Church

A church-based ministry may have slightly different priorities. When making a ministry plan for your church, keep in mind the following program elements:

- ☐ Sunday school classes for people with intellectual disabilities
- ☐ Family night classes/activities for people with intellectual disabilities
- ☐ Transportation for people with disabilities

- ☐ Pastoral counseling
- ☐ Visitation and felt-needs ministry
- ☐ Support and fellowship groups outside the church itself (such as a Special Touch Chapter) that can assist in providing parental, spousal, and other caregiver support
- ☐ Short-term respite care
- ☐ Friendship building

The above list is simply an example of *some* of the programs a church might offer to its congregation and community. Every local church and community will be different, and each will have slightly different needs. In addition to these specific ministries, care must be taken that people with disabilities are not neglected in the routine life of the church, which includes worship, fellowship activities, and ministry gift development.

Recruit Facilitators

Sometimes a church's disability ministry can become isolated from the rest of its outreaches to the community because it is the pet project of just a few people. This usually happens because of the false perception that disability ministry requires a specialist who has knowledge or experience in the area of disability. Although knowledge and experience can be helpful, they are never a requirement. Every person in every pew has a gift or talent that can be used to bless and reach people with disabilities for Christ if they simply have a willing heart. You have to have this philosophy if you are going to successfully recruit workers and helpers to your ministry and create a broad base of support and awareness throughout the congregation. The entire church body is your potential ministry team. Disability ministry needs everything from plumbers to pastry chefs at one time or another; it is a ministry in which everyone, at almost any age, can participate. Learn how to plug the right person, with the right ministry gift, into the right ministry opportunity.

CREATING AN ATMOSPHERE OF LOVE AND ACCEPTANCE

In order to create an atmosphere of love and acceptance, we first have to recognize that a gulf often exists between the world of the church and the world of people living with disabilities.

Understand the World of the Church

The world of the church has certain inherent characteristics:

☐ The life of the church centers around celebrating Jesus, worshipping God, and fellowshipping with the saints

☐ By design, the church is a family unit

☐ Sunday services often showcase the church at its best

Even though these things are good, when viewed from the perspective of people with disabilities, they can become problematic.

Understand the World of People with Disabilities

The world of disability has unique characteristics that put it at odds with the church. They are:

☐ People with disabilities often feel betrayed by God or isolated from Him; therefore they are not sure about worship. They wrestle with the question, "If God is so loving and so powerful, Why did He allow this terrible thing to happen to me?"

☐ In a group of able-bodied people, people with disabilities often feel isolated and ignored—not part of the family.

☐ Some people with disabilities are continually confronted with the base side of life. They often feel uncomfortable and uneasy about their appearance and behaviors. They know that they may seem bizarre or revolting to others.

A quick comparison and analysis of these of characteristics illuminate the problems. *If people with a disability feel that God has punished or rejected them, and think they are an accident or a mistake, why should they want to go to God's house and celebrate Him?* Going to church can feel like attending someone else's family reunion. It is a closed circle. The smiles and hugs are for those who are known and loved. Only those in the family know the inside jokes. Strangers are treated with cool politeness. Why should a person with a disability confront the logistical hassles of going to church and being lonely when they can be lonely at home? Even people without disabilities often feel this way.

The next issue you must face can be very difficult. Is the church— *your* church—ready for the stark ugliness of some of the things that accompany disability? Are you ready for drool on your upholstery and seizures on your floor? Are you ready to help empty a leg bag that needs immediate attention? Is your pastor prepared for those who may interact with his sermon by answering his rhetorical questions or by interjecting irrelevancies, or fall obviously and noisily asleep? Are you prepared to deal with people who may not look pretty, dress pretty, smell pretty, or act pretty? Most people with disabilities don't think so, and that is why the statistics say that they are staying away from the church in droves. *The average Sunday service often unwittingly celebrates appearance and ability, which is a mark of the worldly culture in which we live. Our culture is often highly intolerant of physical and mental imperfection.* The final result is that people with disabilities can feel the church has placed a "KEEP OUT!" sign on the front door of their accessible, multi-million dollar facility. If we take this perspective into serious consideration, is it any wonder why the master of the banquet instructed His servants to compel the maimed, lame, and blind to come in? (Luke 14:23)

The Solution

During the youth revival of the 1970's, some churches were literally home-grown. They began as home Bible studies and grew to number in the thousands. There were also established churches that experienced phenomenal growth. Whether they knew it or not, these churches put biblical principles into practice causing them to reap a tremendous harvest of souls. Practicing these same principles will energize your disability outreach and your entire church.

Be Consumed by the Love of Christ

Members and adherents of those churches experienced a personal revival. They were personally so touched by the love of God that they were filled with a burning desire to share it with friends, enemies, and everyone they encountered, without regard for personal inconvenience.

> *This is how God showed his love among us: He sent his one and only Son into the world that we might live through him. This is love: not that we loved God, but that he loved us and sent his Son as an atoning sacrifice for our sins. Dear friends, since God so loved us, we also ought to love one another. No one has ever seen God; but if we love each other, God lives in us and his love is made complete in us.* (1 John 4:9-12 NIV)

Have One Agenda

These churches were not mired down in formality, frigidity, politics or petty bickering. They were not perfect, but they were motivated by a single agenda that overshadowed and impacted everything they did. The love that surged through them compelled them to carry out Christ's Great Commission in Mark 16:15 to preach the Good News and make disciples. *They were especially attracted to those in their communities who were alienated or disenfranchised.*

Be Willing to Alter Your Practices Accordingly

Because the Great Commission dictated everything these churches did, people were willing to go beyond their comfort zones to make people feel welcome. They never compromised biblical values, but they relaxed traditions and radically changed their manner of worship to make room in the family of God for the people that were being drawn to Jesus. Specifics varied because every situation was unique, but the substance of this step involves having a tender spirit, a compassionate heart, and a willing attitude.

> *Let nothing be done through selfish ambition or conceit, but in lowliness of mind let each esteem others better than himself. Let each of you look*

out not only for his own interests, but also for the interests of others. (Phil. 2:3-4)

Accessible churches start with accessible hearts.
Accessible hearts declare, "Whoever comes to me I will never
drive away."
(John 6:37 NIV)

Show Your Sensitivity through Your Language

In welcoming people with disabilities into the family of God, a congregation needs to become educated in the use of culturally correct terminology when speaking to, or about, people with disabilities. Although it may seem petty to those outside the community of people with disabilities, within the sub-culture it is an extremely important and sensitive issue. Language impacts the way that people are perceived or defined. People with disabilities are far more than the sum of their weaknesses or their hardware. For example, it is no more appropriate to call a person in a wheelchair a "wheelchair" than it is to call a person who drives a car an "automobile." People with disabilities want to be defined as *people first*.

There are several words that are currently considered arcane, and should never be used. They include, among others, *crippled, handicapped*, and *deformed*. Words like *retarded* and *defect* should be used sparingly, carefully, and only in a clinical context. *Handicapable* is also arcane. *Physically challenged* and *mentally challenged* are passé, but are usually considered inoffensive.

It is also very important that the terms *mental disability* and *learning disability* are not used interchangeably. The term mental disability or disabilities is generally used when discussing mental retardation. The term learning disability or disabilities is commonly used when referring to learning disorders such as Dyslexia, Dysgraphia, ADD and ADHD among others, that are usually not related to mental retardation. For example, Thomas Edison was dyslexic, but he was not mentally retarded. These respective terms represent two different kinds of problems and are definitely not synonymous. Terms that can be used along with mental disability currently include *intellectual disability* and *cognitive delay*. It is advisable to stay current on language usage because, in all probability, it will continue to change over time.

Correct language usage will help your church and its disability ministry:

- ☐ It demonstrates you are credible in that you care enough to be informed and act accordingly.
- ☐ It demonstrates compassion and sensitivity.
- ☐ It helps you earn the right to be heard.

If we choose *not* to use the correct language, some people with disabilities may turn us off and dismiss our message as irrelevant before we even get started. For many people who do not live with a disability, this language issue may seem petty and trivial, but the mission of the church calls us to see life through the eyes of those whom we serve. Paul stated, "to the weak I became weak, to win the weak. I have become all things to all men so that by all possible means I might save some" (1 Cor. 9:22 NIV).

The use of the phrase "the disabled" is discouraged because it communicates uselessness and worthlessness and defines an individual as "broken."
Example: A "disabled" car is unable to function.

CREATE AN UNDERSTANDING OF THE NEED FOR ACCESSIBLE FACILITIES

Educating people about accessibility is important. Many older churches were built when the majority of people with disabilities had a homebound lifestyle. Even some newer churches and Christian facilities are inaccessible even though they may have been "built to code" but did not pre-test their building dimensions with real people who use walkers and wheelchairs. There is a Christian retreat center in the Midwest that had to pay for an expensive "do over" because they installed roll in showers without pre-testing.

Accessible facilities demonstrate the concern, compassion, and commitment of the church in a visible and practical way. Creating understanding of the need for accessible facilities involves education and evaluation.

Educate

Devise creative ways of educating your congregation, pastoral staff, and board members about the importance of accessibility. Get your core group together for a brainstorming session on ways to increase accessibility awareness in your congregation.

Accessibility Awareness Tip:

Have your core group strap your pastoral staff and deacon board into wheel-chairs and take them on a tour of the church, simulating as many disabilities as possible. Have them try to manipulate themselves in a wheelchair throughout the entire building.

Accommodation

A common misconception about disability ministry is that it requires a considerable financial investment in order to begin. It does not! This does not mean disability ministry is cheap; it is not! To be effective, it demands tremendous investments of time, energy, and prayer. It requires a commitment to servanthood and evangelism, and it will stretch you by taking you far beyond your comfort zone. It is true that sooner or later money will come into play, *but any church, regardless of their financial situation, can start a disability ministry by adopting a policy of accommodation.* An accommodation policy is simply a commitment to do whatever it takes to include people with disabilities in the full life of the church. All that is required is a compassionate heart, some ingenuity, and a few strong backs. *Accommodation should always be seen as a first step toward complete accessibility and never as an end in itself.*

Accommodation Tip:

Carrying people in wheelchairs up and down stairs can be dangerous for everyone involved. Relocate Sunday school classes with students in wheelchairs to rooms with easy accessibility.

Evaluate Accessibility

Analyze the various areas of your church for accessibility. Do this by asking some key questions. Below is a sample assessment that you may adapt for your own unique situation.

PARKING LOT

Marked Parking Stalls

1. Are they wide enough? Will they accommodate a van with a wheelchair lift out the side of the vehicle?
2. Are they on level ground?
3. Are they obstacle free?
4. Are they properly reserved and visible with an accessibility icon?
5. Are they near a curb breakout?
6. Are they near an accessible entry?
7. Is there an attendant available to aid those who may require assistance?
8. Is parking monitored to keep disability parking free for those who truly need it?

Entrances

1. Is there a carport or awning?
2. Does the carport or awning have sufficient clearance?
3. Is there at least one accessible entryway?
4. Is it conveniently located?
5. If not, is the route to the accessible entrance clearly marked?
6. Are there stairs? If so, are they ramped or attended?
7. Are the doorways wide enough to accommodate people in wheelchairs?
8. Is the accessible entrance attended?

Accessibility to Other Levels

1. Are elevators or wheelchair lifts in proper repair and ready for use?

2. If a key is needed for use of an elevator or wheel chair lift, are there clearly posted instructions explaining how one can obtain the key?

3. Are there attendants to escort people with disabilities through alternate routes?

Traffic Patterns

1. Can people in wheelchairs maneuver freely to the sanctuary and other rooms?

2. Can they sit without blocking aisles and entryways?

Restrooms

1. Is there one gender-neutral bathroom available so caregivers of a different gender are able to provide assistance?

2. Are the doors wide enough for people in wheelchairs?

3. Do the doors swing in the right direction?

4. Are the stalls wide enough for people in wheelchairs?

5. Are they equipped with grab bars? Are there handles on both sides of the stall doors?

6. Are sinks, faucets, soap, towels and mirrors accessible to people in wheelchairs?

7. Are restrooms labeled with large print signs for the visually impaired and Braille markings for those who are blind?

Sunday School Classrooms

1. Are these rooms accessible to people in wheelchairs?

2. Is the seating arranged to facilitate people in wheelchairs?

3. Has an effective environment, free of unnecessary distractions, been prepared in classrooms for people with intellectual disabilities?

The Sanctuary

1. Does the seating plan provide seating space for people in wheelchairs?

2. Are large print Bibles, hymnals, and chorus sheets available for the visually impaired?

3. Are there amplification devices for the hearing impaired?

4. Is sign language provided for those from the deaf culture?

5. Is the platform accessible (either permanently or as needed) for pulpit guests or platform personnel with disabilities?

General

1. Do you have an accessible telephone and drinking fountain?

2. Are your ushers/attendants trained in proper disability etiquette, assistance, and emergency procedures?

Accessibility Tip:
Never build or remodel without pre-testing building accessibility specifications with the help of people in wheelchairs.

FIT INTO THE FLOW

Every church has a particular way they do things. There is an administrative scheme or flow that establishes responsibilities, expectations, and lines of accountability for every ministry program in the church. Such a scheme can be very formal with written policies and procedures or very informal, based on unwritten church customs and traditions. Every church is a unique situation. You and your core group need to communicate with your pastor and find out where your ministry fits into the administrative flow of the church, and what your specific lines of accountability are.

A Suggested Flow of Administration

Pastor > Board > Christian Ed. Dir. > Disability Ministry
Coordinator > Asst. Coordinator > Workers

Ministry Leadership Responsibilities

The ministry coordinator should be prepared to:

☐ Work with the pastor, C. E. Director, and the disability ministry core group to map out the ministry plan discussed earlier.

☐ Plan and oversee all ministry activities.

☐ Have a strategy for worker recruitment and training.

☐ Track growth and maintain an evangelistic focus.

☐ Be a "troubleshooter," act as a liaison between workers and other church departments, and handle possible programming and/or personality conflicts.

The Essence of Leadership

In Christian circles it is often said, that effective leadership begins on its knees. In disability ministry, that phrase is especially apt in another way. It is significant that one of the last object lessons Jesus taught to the very first ministry core group was servanthood. Jesus was the first one to pick up the towel (John 13). On one level, effective leadership in disability ministry can be measured by who is the first one to the gloves, the talk board, the urinal, or the home of a shut-in. Workers serve better when they are served by leaders who model servanthood as if it were a suit of clothes.

Take a Christ-like Approach to Change

In an editorial commentary, Charlie Chivers, Executive Director of Special Touch Ministry, Inc., made the following observations about the attitude one should have when trying to precipitate change in a local church:

It is important, as we strive to make changes in our churches, that we maintain the right spirit. We can become so rabid for change that we unconsciously adopt "the end justifies the means" attitude. A friend once gave me some wise counsel. "Charlie, those who ride the white charger of disability ministry must be careful not to impale people on their lance." Change cannot be forced upon people; it must be built in them.

I have found a simple formula for building change - a formula that has been a nationwide craze. It is expressed in the letters "WWJD?" which stands for, "What Would Jesus Do?" This is neither a slick marketing slogan, nor a namby-pamby, turn-the-other-cheek philosophy. It is a guidance principle based on the only perfect example we have ever been given. When we face difficult issues, asking ourselves this simple question will help us function with pure motives and a right spirit.

Jesus used many different methods, in many different circumstances, to evoke change. He made it His first responsibility to understand the nature of the beast He was trying to tame. Only then did He determine the approach He would take. Choosing the right approach may win you unexpected allies. Jesus evoked change in the lives of prostitutes and priests, peasants and the social elite, farmers, fishermen, and tax collectors, learned men and women, and even children. He approached each group with *different* methods, yet His approach to all was the same. It was tempered by Love, Truth, and the Word of God. So let's put down our lance, and try a Christ-like approach to change.

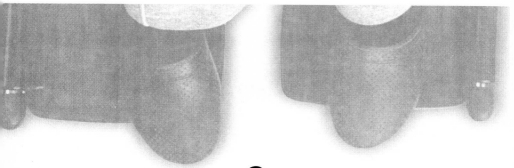

2.
Compel Them to Come In: A Winning Strategy for Evangelism

Objectives

- ☐ To learn the Biblical method for bringing in people with disabilities
- ☐ To become a servant
- ☐ To find and identify people with disabilities in your community
- ☐ To earn the right to be heard
- ☐ To offer a compelling program
- ☐ To provide functionally appropriate programming

The Concept

In the majority of cases, people with disabilities will not seek out your church. You will have to seek *them* out.

Foundation Scriptures

Luke 14:12-14; 21, 23

Learn the Biblical Method

A study of the parable of the great feast in Luke 14 gives us an approach to the problem of bringing people with disabilities into our midst.

When you give a dinner or a supper, do not ask your friends, your brothers, your relatives, nor your rich neighbors, lest they also invite you back, and you be repaid. But when you give a feast, invite the poor, the maimed, the lame, the blind. And you will be blessed, because they cannot repay you; for you shall be repaid at the resurrection of the just. (vv. 12-14)

Go out quickly into the streets and lanes of the city, and bring in here the poor and the maimed and the lame and the blind. . . .Go out into the highways and hedges, and compel them to come in, that my house may be filled. (vv. 21, 23)

Although they do not appear in this order, a breakdown of this passage reveals the following elements:

- ☐ Go out beyond your walls (vv. 21, 23).
- ☐ Go as a servant (v. 17).
- ☐ Seek out those who are in need (vv. 13, 21).
- ☐ Canvass your community (vv. 21, 23).
- ☐ Meet felt needs (v. 12).
- ☐ Compel them to come in (v. 23).
- ☐ Do it now (v. 21).

To Become a Servant Go as a Servant

In this parable, the first thing the master of the feast did was to dispatch his servants. As we prepare to minister to people with disabilities, we need to check our attitudes and motives. Evangelist Gary Pratt once challenged an audience by saying, "When it comes to serving Jesus Christ, do you want a title or a towel?" Many of us long to be *somebody* with a great ministry, but we feel like we need to be able to preach a masterful sermon, or sing an inspiring song in order to be effective. The truth is Jesus taught that effective ministry happens when we forget ourselves, forget about *being somebody*, and pick up the towel and start washing feet. Servanthood takes us out of the equation and puts the focus where it belongs—on Jesus and on others. A true servant has a powerful ministry in Christ because he has the mind and heart of Christ. To a true servant, no task is too demeaning, and no person is unworthy of time and attention. Jesus said, "*Whoever desires to be great among you shall be your servant. And whoever of you desires to be first shall be slave of all*" (Mark 10:43-44). We are also instructed to "Bear one another's burdens and so fulfill the law of Christ" (Gal. 6:2).

"Its not about you, it's about Jesus" (Ron Auch).

FIND AND IDENTIFY PEOPLE WITH DISABILITIES IN YOUR COMMUNITY

This objective entails four elements from the parable.

Go Out Beyond Your Own Walls

Whether they intend to or not, most churches make their facilities accessible for the comfort and convenience of their current members and adherents. A 1995 survey of a major evangelical fellowship found that only eight percent of their churches were engaged in any type of outreach to people with disabilities. Of that number, less than half were reaching beyond their own walls. It was said earlier, but it needs to be mentioned again here, the majority of people with disabilities cannot or will not come to you. Many are isolated, immobile, or both. Many won't come because they are intimidated or insecure. It cannot be emphasized enough that *you have to go to them*.

Seek Out Those Who Are in Need; Canvass Your Community

These two elements overlap. You can find and make contact with people with disabilities by blanketing your community, or in larger cities, your vicinity. Divide your "targets" into two groups: people who live in institutionalized settings (hospitals, rehab centers, nursing homes and community-based residential facilities), and people who live independently.

Tips on Making Contact with People Living in Institutionalized Settings

☐ Always make first contact with an institution through the administration or head chaplain.

☐ Most hospitals and rehab centers will let you post ministry/church information on their bulletin boards.

☐ Many institutions have rotating in-house chapel programs in which your church can participate by providing music and sharing in the Word once a month. These programs allow you to fellowship informally with residents before and after the service.

☐ Some institutions will allow you to set up your own regular weekly Bible studies or Sunday school class.

☐ Offer to provide transportation to residents who are interested in attending church services and special functions.

☐ Always be courteous and cooperative with residence staff. Treat your ministry opportunity on their turf as a privilege. Always ask permission before visiting rooms of individual residents.

☐ Make sure you stay within any time limits you are given.

☐ *The key to success in this type of ministry is consistency. Be there on time; be there every time.*

Program Ideas

- ☐ Bring guitars. Some places have keyboards available. Do not use drums.

- ☐ Services may include singing, special music or a testimony, prayer requests, and a short message.

- ☐ It takes advance planning, but give residents opportunities to share special music and testimonies in their residence and in your church.

- ☐ Utilize children and teens in special services and for seasonal events like caroling.

Tips on Making Contact with People Living Independently

- ☐ Advertise using radio, TV, web pages, and print media. Use the accessibility icon in your advertising.

- ☐ Canvass door-to-door to publicize a special church event or a courtesy service, such as transportation to and from the church, offered by your disability ministry. Look for ramps on homes and other indicators which signal that people with disabilities live in a home. Carry church information and gospel tracts or music tapes with you to leave with them.

- ☐ Get visitation referrals from church members.

- ☐ Visit sheltered workshops and leave ministry information.

- ☐ Some independent living apartment complexes have rotating Bible studies. They also have bulletin boards where you could leave information or free bus passes.

- ☐ Make your ministry available to Special Olympics, camps, and other programs or disability organizations.

These are just some suggestions on canvassing your community. Get your core group together and have them brainstorm on how your disability ministry can take advantage of the unique features of your particular community.

The Purpose of Canvassing and Home Visitation

Many evangelical churches do canvassing and home visitation as part of their weekly regimen for the purpose of sharing the gospel. Usually the approach such teams take is very direct. A person opens their door and is confronted with, "Good evening, we're from First Church, and we'd like to know if you know Jesus Christ as your personal Lord and Savior, because if you DO, you get to go to HEAVEN, but if you DON'T you're goin' to HELL! Excuse me, but do I smell something BURNING?!"

A softer, more subtle approach needs to be used *because your purpose is not only to lead them to Christ, but to build a long-term relationship with them.* The tone behind your words must be completely different. No matter how you frame your greeting, what you want them to hear is, "Good evening, we're from First Church, *is there anything we can do to help?"*

We are not trying to minimize the value of spontaneous ministry. If you do this long enough, you will encounter many crisis situations where you will be asked to minister immediately. However, in most situations, people are frightened by strangers who display excessive zeal.

Tips on Initial Home Visitation

Every home visit is a unique situation, especially if it is the result of a referral. Here are some general guidelines for visitation procedures and etiquette when making your first contact with someone.

- ☐ Always do visitation with a partner. Have a neat appearance. *Presentation is everything.*

- ☐ It's a good idea to represent a church event such as a concert, VBS, or a ministry such as bus pickup. Representing an event is much less threatening than simply witnessing door to door. Representing a church program or event communicates the message: "Can we help?" Simply witnessing door to door can be perceived as communicating the message: "There is something fundamentally wrong with you, and we are here to enlighten you and show you the truth."

- □ Don't be argumentative or judgmental about *anything*. At this point, it doesn't matter what they are doing, saying, hearing, or watching.

- □ Be upbeat. Be brief.

- □ Ask if you or a pastor may call again.

- □ Ask if there is a prayer need for which you can pray while you are with them and/or take with you to place on a prayer chain.

- □ Leave an information packet and some type of gospel literature or a music tape.

- □ Follow up the following week. Make sure to ask about the prayer need.

Do it Now

In the parable in Luke 14, the master of the feast urged his servants to "go quickly." He didn't want them to get bogged down in strategy sessions and motivational meetings. Their motivation was his order to go out. Their strategy was to do what he said, "Go out into the streets and the lanes and the highways and the hedges." There are good reasons to start reaching out immediately. *Do something now, no matter how small your core group is.*

- □ Disability ministry is a "last days ministry," and salvation is a limited time offer. As our worldly society continues to deteriorate, people with disabilities will need the protection of the local church.

- □ Many people with disabilities, of all ages and disability types, are physically frail and will have a shorter than average life span. In spiritual terms, they represent fruit that is literally dying on the vine.

- □ Robert Schuller, the great preacher and motivational speaker, once said, "Beginning is half done." Starting now, and getting some positive outreach experience behind you produces momentum. Plus almost every effort at outreach, no matter how minimal, has a ripple effect that will impact people you don't even know. *A good rule of thumb is, "Do it. Do it right. Do it right now!"*

Earn the Right to Be Heard

Joni Erickson Tada states that the reason she is a Christian today is because the people who shared Jesus with her after her diving accident "earned the right to be heard." They didn't look at her as a notch to be carved on their gospel gun. They took time to build a relationship. They played Monopoly. They read books. They watched old movies. They talked. They invested time and energy in building a friendship. When Joni believed her friends, whom she could see, truly cared about her, she could believe that Jesus, whom she couldn't see, also cared about her. Love is the key, and love is spelled T-I-M-E.

Some people sneer at this method as soft-pedaling the gospel. It is not. It's taking the gospel into the lives of people. Building relationships builds trust. Many people impacted by disability have had their trust abused in the name of religion. As stated in the previous chapter, they don't trust God because they wrestle with the question, "If God is an all powerful God who loves me and has a good plan for my life, how could He allow this terrible thing to happen?" While there are theological answers to that question, the flesh and blood answer is a face-to-face encounter with absolute, irresistible love that transcends normal human experience. If you know Jesus, then you are His love with skin on (see Rom. 5:5), and an encounter with you can become an encounter with Him—but you have to earn the right to be heard.

Jesus modeled relationship building evangelism. He sat down and ate with those who were considered the dregs of society (Matt. 9:10-13; Luke 7:34). He sought out and ministered to the Samaritan woman who represented a group of people the Jews hated (John 4:7-34). He deliberately interacted with and praised a woman who was rejected by the establishment (Luke 7:36-50). He earned the right to be heard.

Meet Felt Needs

Part of relationship building is meeting what are often referred to as *felt needs*. They are called felt needs because we feel deprived when they are not being met. Felt needs include all of the physical, emotional, and social needs a human being can have, from a leaky roof to an empty pantry, feelings of insecurity, and the need to belong. In the parable of the Great Feast, the object of the feast was to give the participants an opportunity to celebrate their relationship with the master, but the feast also met their felt needs for food and fellowship.

**Meeting felt needs MUST be kept in eternal perspective.
Keep focused on the ultimate goal—leading them to Christ,
otherwise meeting felt needs may become a vicious circle without
a greater redemptive purpose.
Meeting felt needs is ALWAYS a means to an end and NEVER an
end in itself.**

The Importance of Felt-Needs Ministry

Felt-needs ministry is vital because:

☐ Meeting practical, social, and emotional needs makes a personal connection with an individual.

☐ It demonstrates personal and divine compassion - which is caring enough about a person's needs to do something to make their situation better.

☐ Meeting felt needs demonstrates commitment to a long-term relationship between the person with a disability and the church.

☐ Meeting felt needs makes our statements about our faith relevant.

What does it profit, my brethren, if someone says he has faith but does not have works? Can faith save him? If a brother or sister is naked and destitute of daily food, and one of you says to them, "Depart in peace, be warmed and filled," but you do not give them the things which are needed for the body, what does it profit? Thus also faith by itself, if it does not have works, is dead. But someone will say, "You have faith, and I have works." Show me your faith without your works, and I will show you my faith by my works. . . . Do you see that faith was working together with his works, and by works faith was made perfect? . . . You see then that a man is justified by works, and not by faith only. . . . For as the body without the spirit is dead, so faith without works is dead also. (James 2:14-26)

Examples of Felt-Needs Ministry

An exhaustive list is impossible, but here are three types of this kind of ministry:

- ☐ *A socially-based fellowship* including church-based large groups, small groups, and one-on-one activities that can range from kayaking to chess and from going out for a Coke to a week at a Special Touch Summer Get Away.

- ☐ *A spiritually-based fellowship* such as worship services, Sunday school classes, small groups, and one-on-one Bible studies and/or prayer times.

- ☐ Practical needs assistance may include helping with laundry, home repair, yard work, housekeeping, meal preparation, and respite home health care. Some of these tasks can be handled by connecting individuals to their local County Health and Human Services. However, you will probably encounter people who are on the county's waiting list. People can wait for county services up to five years or even longer.

The Dangers of Felt-Needs Ministry

There are three "red flag" areas in regard to felt-needs ministry:

1. Some church disability ministries end up losing spiritual focus and concentrate all of their energies on taking care of felt needs. Jesus met felt needs when He turned the water into wine and fed the 5,000, etc., but His actions always served the higher spiritual purpose of bringing people into the kingdom of God.

2. In some cases, meeting felt needs fosters an unhealthy dependency on an individual or individuals who are helping, and the person receiving help disengages from the problem-solving process in their life.

3. People involved in helping can become victims of emotional manipulation.

The answer to these problems is to continue to meet felt needs by ministering to every person as unto Christ but doing so with discernment.

Learn the Signs of Manipulation and Unhealthy Dependency

☐ An unwillingness on the part of the person with a disability to accept and exercise reasonable personal responsibility

☐ A subtle but prevailing ingratitude

☐ An attitude of surrender to circumstances

☐ A prevailing feeling on your part that you can never do enough

Manipulation is the dark side of the survival instinct that people with disabilities are taught. Often it is a result of not having healthy relationships. Sometimes a person simply has a controlling, inhospitable, self-centered disposition. People have unique personalities, and background experiences shape their personalities. Due to the darkened nature of the unregenerate heart, not every person with a disability is going to be likable, especially those who don't know Jesus.

Unhealthy dependency upon those who care and provide help is different than manipulation. It is a type of emotional and spiritual exhaustion that comes as a result of being beat up by the demands of living with a disability day in and day out. It is triggered when one is being worn out and overwhelmed and all coping mechanisms have been depleted. From the perspective of a person with a disability, the disability has become an overbearing, out-of-control bully, and he or she has been diminished to nothing as an individual.

The Response to Manipulation and Unhealthy Dependence

The positive side of manipulation and unhealthy dependence is an opportunity for ministry that goes deeper than meeting relatively superficial needs. In both cases, you must be gentle but firm. In the case of manipulation, point out that people are not doormats. The guideline here is to share what the Holy Spirit lays on your heart. You need to understand that some individuals will abuse your ministry and friendship in order to test your Christianity.

In the case of unhealthy dependency:

☐ Be timely. If you have seen the situation develop over a period of three to six months, take action as soon as you feel it will be received. People in this state are usually totally blind to the reality of their situation.

☐ Be honest. Explain your concern, and compassionately point out areas where they have become negligent in personal care and hygiene, personal finance, and relationships.

☐ Be encouraging. Share Christ's ability to empower and restore them; He can help them live proactive lives.

☐ Be practical. Help them to get help in their areas of need. Help them establish lines of accountability with you or others so that the unhealthy dependency does not recur.

☐ Be reassuring. Enfold them in the fail-proof love of Christ that never wavers. Very likely, they will feel embarrassed and ashamed. They will believe they have let their friends and loved ones down. In short, they will feel like failures and will want to retreat into themselves. Your faithfulness to them at this point can help them turn a tailspin into a triumph. Let them know that their willingness to confront the problem is the beginning of something better. Help them understand that down does not mean out. Express your love for them.

☐ Be absolutely confidential.

☐ Be watchful for recurrences. *Their disability isn't going anywhere. They live with it 24/7. In time it will probably beat them up and wear them out again.*

Offer a Compelling Program

"Compel Them to Come In"

The word *compel* means to force, coerce, insist, demand, or require as an irresistible necessity. In effect, the master of the feast directed his servants to *strong arm* his guests. He was not going to take no for an answer; he ordered his servants to find the guests and essentially put them under arrest!

The master of the feast made a deliberate decision to make the outcasts and discards of society his honored guests. For a moment, put yourself in the place of the poor, the lame, and the blind who were suddenly invited to this grand celebration. Some of these people were homeless. Some may have been confused mentally. In all probability, none of them had fashionable or appropriate clothing to wear. What do you think their concerns were? What assurances would they need before allowing themselves to be taken into a foreign environment where they would be completely vulnerable? There is no way to know for certain, but they may have struggled with the following questions:

- ☐ Will I be accepted as I am?
- ☐ Will I be comfortable in that setting?
- ☐ Does the master really care about someone like me?

Many churches have developed program features to draw in people with disabilities. One church literally has a banquet every month for their senior citizens and people with disabilities. That church and others operate bus programs and have concerts and special events. Imagination and resources can help, but your church does not have to be of great size. It does not need a lot of money. Compelling them to come in goes back to basics. It's a people-loving people ministry. If your church can answer "Yes!" to the three basic questions above, then you can compel them to come in. *The Jesus People Church in Minneapolis grew to thousands in the 1970's, mostly from an influx of teens and street people because that church could answer the above three questions in the affirmative.*

PROVIDE FUNCTIONALLY APPROPRIATE PROGRAMMING

Different Approaches to Programming

There are basically three approaches to ministering to people with intellectual disabilities through Sunday school and worship services.

An Integrated Program

This approach is also commonly referred to as mainstreaming or inclusion. The advantage is that people with cognitive delays are kept with individuals their own age. It teaches children how to accept those whom they may view as different.

The disadvantage of an integrated program is that students with a cognitive delay can become intellectually lost and isolated. They fit in only on a superficial level, if they fit in at all. The gravest danger is that they may not be able to understand the gospel presentation.

A Separated or Segregated Program

In a separated program, those with intellectual disabilities become a church within the church. They have their own Sunday school class, worship service, and activities. The advantages of a separated program are that people with intellectual disabilities receive teaching at their level with love and understanding from those who accept them as they are.

The main disadvantage is that they are cut off from the rest of the body. They run the risk of never being completely assimilated into the family of God and the full life of the church. As a result, the church will never have the opportunity to benefit from their gifts.

A Combination of Both

Combining the integrated and segregated approaches eliminates the disadvantages of both. There are times when people with intellectual disabilities need to be a part of the corporate body, and there are times when they need to be separated in order to receive specialized ministry.

Special Touch Ministry has had tremendous success with keeping the whole body together for praise and worship, and then separating the two groups before the message so that each can receive ministry at their appropriate level. In a church setting, you would also have everyone together for fellowship meals, picnics, etc. It is vital for those with cognitive disabilities to know that they are a valued part of a larger whole.

Functionally Appropriate Programming

In order to effectively use the remainder of this guide, you must understand that functionally appropriate programming and dependence on the Holy Spirit are the keys to effectively reaching people with intellectual disabilities. This approach respects the diversity of their learning styles and cognitive levels. People with intellectual disabilities fall into three general cognitive levels: severe and profound (0-6 years in mental age), low functioning (7-11 years), and high functioning (12 years and up). To be effective, your ministry will need to offer programming designed to accommodate these three groups.

The concept of functionally appropriate programming is founded upon the conviction that every person is entitled to a presentation of the gospel at his or her level of comprehension.

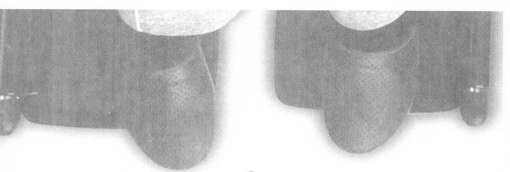

3.

Presenting the Need: How to plan a Disability Awareness Sunday

OBJECTIVES

- ☐ To learn to qualify the need
- ☐ To present the need and educate the congregation
- ☐ To create opportunities for social interaction between people with disabilities and the congregation
- ☐ To articulate the biblical imperatives and make a spiritual application
- ☐ To identify possible program options

THE CONCEPT

To fulfill the Great Commission, it is necessary to mobilize the church. The church is mobilized when information is presented on the foundation of biblical imperatives and a congregation is motivated to present Christ to people with disabilities in their community.

Foundation Scripture

James 1:27

INTRODUCTION

A Disability Awareness Sunday can be a milestone in the life and vitality of the local church. Unfortunately, this event too often becomes a token offering to fulfill an obligatory date on the annual church calendar and appease a few vocal constituents with disability ministry concerns. This would include Disability Ministry coordinators, special needs Sunday school teachers, and those individuals and families directly impacted by physical or mental disability on a daily basis. These two groups of people, one with a lonely ministry call and the other with a daily cross to bear, are often disenfranchised from the body. They feel unnoticed and unwanted because they ride an unpopular "hobby horse" that makes others uncomfortable. They are rarely included or considered in the overall planning of the church.

For some reason, reaching people with disabilities is the unwanted stepchild of church ministries. Here are some facts for consideration:

☐ When building renovations are made, the building committee or architectural team rarely consults with Disability Ministry leaders or gets the input of those affected by disability. They don't realize that blindly following state specifications can lead to costly do-overs. (A Christian camp in Illinois had to re-do all the "accessible" bathrooms in their new lodge because no one thought to test the specs with real people in real wheelchairs. The state specs did not take into account needed "turn around" room.)

☐ Major churches sometimes isolate and lose contact with their ministry to people with disabilities. The disability ministry becomes a church within the church that is never visited by the church leadership or the congregation at-large. Workers within the ministry are seldom encouraged.

☐ Members of the disability community within the church are generally overlooked as active participants in church life and ministry. Even though these connections are absolutely vital for people with disabilities, they are virtually ignored when people are recruited for activities such as teaching a Sunday school class, working in the nursery, participating in church dramas and musicals, Sunday school picnics, fellowship, and even work days. Since many people with disabilities have the desire and the skills to perform these functions, this lack of consideration sends silent signals that they are perceived as useless.

When people feel disenfranchised, two things occur. Individuals and families affected by disability react by becoming very private and retreating even further into their own world. Some may appear self-involved, strange, indifferent, unfriendly, and unwilling to fit into the church family. Others will become manipulative, abrupt, and ungrateful, marking themselves as undesirable to be around.

At the same time, disability ministry workers in the church tend to become vocal advocates on behalf of those they serve. They become warriors for their people who are sometimes more than willing to risk being perceived as offensive or belligerent in pursuit of their righteous cause. There is nothing wrong with being an advocate or a warrior, but constant extreme behavior accompanied by continual "harping" can cause one to appear angry, single-minded, deaf, indifferent to the needs and concerns of others, and insubordinate. Such attitudes and tactics will never win the heart of church leadership. They only alienate good people, pushing them away instead of drawing them into supporting the ministry.

"Those who ride the white charger of disability ministry must be careful not to impale people on their lance."

If disability ministry workers become lobbyists, using political muscle within the church to manipulate the pastor into supporting their agenda, then disability ministry ceases to be a worthy outreach and is reduced to a token gesture of political expedience. That kind of pressure leaves a bad taste in the pastor's mouth and triggers a negative emotional response towards ministry to people with disabilities.

The devastating fact is that in *this* ministry emotion is everything! It becomes a major driving force. Not one of us can argue that! Emotion fuels passion! Fostering any type of negative emotion in pastoral leadership or the local constituency of your church must be avoided at all costs. Once that train starts down the wrong track, it will gain so much momentum that only an intervening act of God can turn it around.

If a Disability Ministry Coordinator has a loud and irritating bark, all the church leadership will do is throw the angry dog a bone. Sometimes this bone is called, "Disability Awareness Sunday," a once-a-year token moment in the spotlight so the Disability Ministry Coordinator can ride his or her favorite hobby horse in front of the entire congregation. A Disability Awareness Sunday born out of this spirit only serves to pacify those who already carry the burden. The congregation rarely gets anything more out of the service than a little information and a clean conscience. They listen to an impassioned speaker and give an offering. In this way, they do their bit for people with disabilities for another year and still manage to get out of the service in time to beat the Baptists to the Cracker Barrel restaurant. No one is moved, no one is changed, and certainly, no one is impacted for the Kingdom of God in a lasting way. Year after year this pattern is repeated. Disability ministry spins its wheels, and people in the disability community slip into hell for lack of an outreach.

The way to break this cycle is to develop a real biblical vision for reaching the lost and the disenfranchised. *People with disabilities are lost souls. They are not granted a special dispensation from hell just because everyone feels sorry for them and calls them "special." They need salvation from sin that is found only through Jesus Christ.* Disability ministry is all about maintaining and presenting this vision.

The purpose of Disability Awareness Sunday is to cast this vision before the congregation in order to stir compassion, energize conviction, and issue a call to every man, woman, boy and girl in the church. At the very least, this will create a healthy commitment to the idea of servanthood, and at the very best, it will compel them to roll up their sleeves, pick up the towel, get their hands wet, and wash feet alongside of you.

Qualify the Need

Qualifying the need involves presenting authoritative facts and other evidence to move your congregation toward conviction and action. This is the part of the service in which you give national, state, and local figures about the impact of disability on your world, your nation, your community, and your congregation. You can find up-to-date national statistics on the National Organization on Disability web site. State and local statistics are available through your county Health and Human Services department. Independent Living Centers, Sheltered Workshops, nursing homes, rehab centers and group homes are also sources of statistical information.

Another way of qualifying the need is to spiritualize it by presenting the biblical imperatives. Present people with disabilities as an unreached people group. As noted earlier, Luke 14 provides a mandate, a motivation, and a method for fulfilling the Great Commission. Scripture establishes evangelism as God's highest priority: He is "not willing that any should perish . . .all should come to repentance" (2 Pet. 3:9).

Too many of us view the Great Commission as detached and impersonal. It is not impersonal to God; it is His personal heart's cry. It is a mission of rescue and recovery that was started in the Garden of Eden. It reached its zenith at Calvary and will continue until Christ returns. God's relentless determination to pursue this mission with boundless love was shown by His willingness to sacrifice His only Son. In sending Jesus Christ to the Cross, He demonstrated that Heaven would not be complete without each and every soul that ever lived. Every Christian should ask themselves the question, "Is God's passion, priority, and pursuit of lost souls reflected in my heart's attitude and actions?"

The Church needs to understand the links between the Great Commission, people with disabilities, and individuals in your local congregation. Current figures suggest that one out of every five people will experience some form of disability at some point in their life. In other words, disability will touch virtually every family. The greatest disability of all is to face a Christless eternity, and this future awaits every individual who is not touched and changed by the efforts of Christians to fulfill the Great Commission. That includes our friends, our parents, our brothers and sisters, our children, and our spouse.

The biblical imperative to make a commitment with our life and lifestyle to fulfill the Great Commission in our home, our church, our community, and beyond, needs to be a central thrust when qualifying the need. Caring about disability issues now not only makes us a more compassionate Christian, it prepares us for our own future and that of our loved ones.

The biggest misconception about ministry to people with disabilities is that it requires someone "special."
Every Christian, in every pew, has something they can do to touch someone else with the love of Jesus Christ.

EDUCATE

Presenting statistics and scriptural verses are only the beginning. New knowledge has to be anchored to real-life situations and internalized if it is going to motivate someone to make life-changing decisions and act on them.

It is imperative that Disability Awareness Sunday deliver vital and valuable information to better prepare the congregation for its role in disability ministry. The following core concepts need to be addressed:

- God ordained the sanctity and value of all human life.

- The desire for a sense of self-worth is the most basic, fundamental need in every individual's life.

- Every human being, regardless of their circumstances, deserves respect.

- The community of people with disabilities and the community of people without disabilities are part of a single human family that has more in common than the measure of their differences.

- God's love embraces the variety and diversity of human cultures, experiences, and life situations. God does not exclude anyone from His love on the basis of a human flaw or imperfection. He is no respecter of persons; that means He is without prejudice or discrimination.

Investigating these key issues tends to erase the differences between the disabled and non-disabled cultures and lower the level of fear and distrust. Understanding them neutralizes the "us versus them" dichotomy in our thinking and makes it much more difficult to justify class distinctions of any kind.

The assimilation of this kind of knowledge becomes a godly process. Most prejudice and indifference toward a people group stems from a lack of information about that group and a lack of desire to acquire it. Bible-based knowledge allows us to see ourselves in the light of God's perspective. The book of James compares it to looking into a mirror. Looking into this mirror honestly gives us the capacity to repent and align our attitudes, actions, beliefs and commitments with those of God. When we see disability with vision, understanding, and the realization that, "there, but for the grace of God go I," we are quicker to embrace those we were willing to shun moments earlier. Education leads to identification.

A POINT OF IDENTIFICATION

People need a reason or an opportunity to identify with the life situations of those to whom they've been called to minister. If you fail to help your congregation identify with your ministry, and more importantly, with the people living with disabilities in your ministry, their movement towards an active flow of compassion will be only temporary. Quite possibly it will last only as long as your presentation lasts. After they've dried their tears and gone home to their Sunday meatloaf and the chance to watch the Packers beat the Buffalo Bills, they will forget what the emotion was all about.

We need to make an emotional connection, as opposed to simply raising intellectual awareness, because we're trying to move the congregation to the point of making a commitment to servanthood. When Jesus saw that the multitudes were like sheep without a shepherd, He was moved with compassion. He didn't simply stand by the wayside and weep over their situation. Compassion—His emotional identification with their plight—moved Him to act on their behalf.

Compassion is empathy that rises to the point of being willing to make a difference or change a situation in spite of the personal cost or sacrifice.

People are not easily moved by facts and statistics alone. Facts do not quickly penetrate the heart and soul where empathy develops. As human beings, we are moved more readily when we can identify or empathize with another person. Facts need to be linked with faces and situations. They need to be made real and personal.

Jesus used the story of the Good Samaritan (Luke 10:25-38) to make that linkage. The Good Samaritan had the compassionate heart of a true servant. When he came upon the stranger who had been robbed and left alone by the side of the road to die, he didn't pass by like the others. He stopped and looked into the man's face—a face was probably bloodied and bruised. He would have seen the pain and the fear the man felt. When he looked into those eyes that pled for mercy, an emotional contact was made. At that point the Good Samaritan must have thought, "This poor man could be me." Rather than walking away, he showed mercy and tenderness by pouring healing oil and wine into the wounds to soothe and disinfect them. Then he lifted the beaten man unto his horse and took him to a place of safety. The Good Samaritan invested in this man's life; he financed his recovery, and came back later to check on his progress. This kind of compassionate action resonates in the heart of God, and Jesus said, "Inasmuch as you did it unto one of the least of these my brethren, you did it to Me" (Matt.25: 40).

Here are some suggestions that can help you bring a congregation to a point of identification:

☐ Visual images: slides, videos and the faces of real people with disabilities

☐ Stories of real people in the community; the appearance of special guests

☐ Personal testimonies of some of the people to whom you minister

- Special music or a drama with a disability emphasis presented by people with disabilities or other special guests.

- Scheduling a missionary or representative from Special Touch Ministry, Inc.

Once the point of identification or an emotional bond is made with the congregation, the door will open to the next key component of a successful Disability Awareness Sunday.

Social Interaction

The need for social interaction with people living with disabilities is a key component of disability awareness. It is a biblical mandate, and it provides the setting for the Luke 14 model for ministry (Luke 14:12, 13).

Social interaction builds friendships. Friendship says, "Not only do I like you, but I like to be around you. You are worth my time and my attention." We all know how good it makes us feel when someone likes us enough to choose to become our friend. Can you imagine how it makes someone with a disability feel, especially someone whose disabilities are severe enough to scare everyone else away?

Here are some ways to create social interaction:

- Give a banquet or luncheon for the whole church in honor of people with disabilities.

- Develop church "foster families" for people with disabilities during the Sunday school and worship service hours, for the entire day, and for holidays and special activities.

- Make sure people in the church are aware of the shut-ins among the church family. They should get a visit once a week and receive a sermon tape or other materials. They should also be recognized and remembered on Disability Awareness Sunday, on their birthday, and on Father's Day, and Mother's Day, etc.

SPIRITUAL APPLICATION

Disability Awareness Sunday must have a spiritual foundation and application; it must articulate biblical imperatives from beginning to end. Basing the need for disability ministry on the biblical imperatives is a far more compelling argument for congregational involvement than an emotional plea based on guilt and/or psychological pressure. Those weapons ultimately produce nothing but resentment. On the other hand, the Holy Spirit uses the Word of God as a tool to convict. We know that "All Scripture is God-breathed and is useful for teaching, rebuking, correcting, and training in righteousness so that the man of God may be thoroughly equipped for every good work" (2 Tim. 3:16 NIV).

Your Disability Awareness Sunday must have the Word of God as its foundation and the driving force. Don't base it on social responsibility or the emotion of individual human struggle. Don't base it on your own passion or the immediate needs of a few individuals in your congregation or community. Instead, base it on the clear commands of the Word of God.

As believers, our convictions are crafted by the Word of God. Emotion can be the gateway to commitment. It is a communication aid, but it is not the author of conviction or actions born out of conviction. Emotion can crystallize a desire to serve, but convictions formed as the Word of God takes root in our hearts and lives are the basis for lasting, life-altering decisions.

PRACTICAL PROGRAM OPTIONS

The limits of what a core group can do to effectively present disability awareness are determined only by its imagination and available resources. The demographics, current programs, human resources, and pastoral vision within each unique church situation factors into what a disability awareness emphasis will look like.

Three popular program options are the vignette, Disability Awareness Sunday, and Disability Awareness Week.

The Vignette

This is a brief window of opportunity in a worship service. A vignette generally includes one of the following presentations:

- [ ] The Disability Ministry Coordinator updates the congregation on what the disability ministry of the church is doing at the present time and what their vision is for the future.
- [ ] A person with a disability gives a testimony and sings or plays an instrument.
- [ ] The special needs Sunday school class offers a skit or musical presentation.
- [ ] A missionary or representative from a national disability ministry shares slides or a video and presents their ministry.

Disability Awareness Sunday

A Disability Awareness Sunday takes elements like those listed above and puts them together into one service. The following components may also be added:

- [ ] A disability awareness emphasis in all levels of Sunday school
- [ ] A sermon oriented toward disability awareness
- [ ] A potluck or banquet centered around disability awareness after the service

Disability Awareness Week

Disability Awareness Week can kick off the week prior to Disability Awareness Sunday. The sample schedule below suggests a few of the possible activities you can use to make your congregation more aware of the need to evangelize people with disabilities in your community.

Board Meeting: The pastoral staff and the church board can do an accessibility assessment or an exercise in sensitivity toward people with disabilities by touring the church in a wheelchair or blindfolded.

Midweek:

Adult Bible study: Teaching could be given on understanding the world of disability. The mid-week service could be devoted to mental disability while Sunday school could be devoted to physical disability, or vice versa.

Youth group: The youth could do disability situation role plays, have discussion groups, invite in a teenage guest speaker with a disability, or do a disability ministry-oriented service project for an individual or a group in the community.

Boys program: Go into the community and do a service project for a person with a disability such as yard work, painting, and/or home repair.

Girls program: Do an inside service project for a person with a disability such as cook, clean, wash dishes, bake, and or/interior painting.

Weekend:

Set up a Friday evening concert featuring a Christian artist with a disability. On Saturday morning, do shut-in visitation within your community. On Saturday afternoon, have a carnival and/or craft fair with proceeds going to disability ministry projects. One church that did this raised enough money to rent buses to bring the residents of a group home to Special Touch chapter meetings.

Conduct a Christian Education department training seminar on disability ministry. Complete the week with Disability Awareness Sunday.

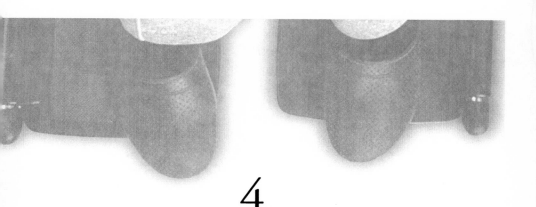

4.

Preparing Your Sunday School to Serve Students with Special Needs

OBJECTIVES

- ☐ To understand the basics of intellectual disability
- ☐ To embrace a philosophy of Christian education that declares that each person deserves a presentation at their level of understanding
- ☐ To learn to create an effective, loving and secure learning environment that facilitates the reception of the gospel message
- ☐ To be able to establish policies and procedures that accommodate disabilities of all types
- ☐ To see that those policies and procedures assure that the fragility, dignity, individuality, spirituality and giftedness of each learner is respected and preserved

THE CONCEPT

Inherent in the Great Commission is the idea that the gospel must be intellectually accessible at all levels of understanding. Jesus rebuked his disciples when they tried to keep children away from Him. People with intellectual disabilities may be of all ages but they have a childlike understanding and deserve unhindered access to their Savior.

Foundation Scripture

Mark 10:13-16

INTRODUCTION

This chapter and the next two deal with ministry to people impacted by intellectual disability. This chapter is largely concerned with preparation and the others provide information on effective presentation. Although the context of those chapters is a worship service, the same principles can be applied to presenting a Sunday School Class.

Intellectual disability is one of a number of terms used to describe what was once commonly referred to as mental retardation. Other currently acceptable terms used to describe this condition are *developmental disability, cognitive delay, cognitive impairment, intellectual impairment, mental disability*, and *learning disability*. The phrase *learning disability* may be technically correct, but it creates confusion when used to describe cognitive delay. It more accurately describes a number of conditions associated with learning difficulties such as dyslexia that do not involve cognitive impairment. Therefore, it unfairly assigns an impairment which they don't have to dyslexics and others. Terms such as *mental handicap* and *mental retardation* are arcane. Although the term mental retardation is still used by the medical community for purposes of assessment and diagnosis, it is misunderstood in other contexts and should be avoided. People with mild intellectual disabilities are also often referred to as *high functioning* when compared with people with moderate or profound intellectual disabilities.

According to *Abnormal Psychology* (2007) by Richard Hilgar and Susan Krauss Whitbourne, intellectual disability or mental retardation exists from childhood and is more common in males. The broad terms above are used to encompass several kinds and levels of mental condition (344).

Our nation's special education law, the Individual with Disabilities Education Act, defines intellectual disability or "mental retardation" as:

> . . . significantly sub-average general intellectual functioning, existing concurrently with deficits in adaptive behavior and

manifested during the developmental period, that adversely affects a child's educational performance." [34 *Code of Federal Regulations* §300.8(c)(6)]

In the context of cognitive delay, intellectual disability can be defined by an IQ score of 75 or less. It is broken down into four sub-categories: profound (IQ below 25), severe (IQ between 25-40), moderate (40-55), and mild (55-70) [Halgin & Krauss Whitbourne 345].

Intellectual disability impacts two general areas of an individual's life: intellectual functioning and adaptive behavior. Adaptive behavior is broken down into three categories: daily living skills, communication skills, and social skills.

According to the website of the National Dissemination Center for Children with Disabilities:

About 87% of people with intellectual disability will only be a little slower than average in learning new information and skills. When they are children, their limitations may not be obvious. They may not even be diagnosed as having intellectual disability until they get to school. As they become adults, many people with intellectual disability can live independently. Other people may not even consider them as having an intellectual disability.

The remaining 13% of people with intellectual disability score below 50 on IQ tests. These people will have more difficulty in school, at home, and in the community. A person with more severe intellectual disability will need more intensive support his or her entire life. Every child with intellectual disability is able to learn, develop, and grow. With help, all children with intellectual disability can live a satisfying life.

Keep in mind that intellectual disability is not a disease; you can't catch it like being exposed to someone with a cold. Neither is it a mental illness like depression (Ibid.). It is a condition that can be caused genetically as in Down Syndrome, environmentally as with Fetal Alcohol Syndrome or through complications in the birthing process. It is also important to note that brain injury can occur through accidents or stroke.

EMBRACE A BIBLICAL PHILOSOPHY OF CHRISTIAN EDUCATION

This is primarily a philosophy of *action*:

- ☐ *Embody* the love of Christ by making a quality decision to unconditionally love those in your classroom regardless of their background, appearance or disability (John 15:9-14).

- ☐ *Model* this decision by way of a lifestyle of Christian love in your classroom.

- ☐ Always remember the foundation of this philosophy is that each person deserves a presentation of the gospel at their level of understanding.

CREATING AN EFFECTIVE, LOVING AND SECURE LEARNING ENVIRONMENT

Adapting a Biblical philosophy is the first key to creating an effective and loving environment. Another way of being effective is to use the right tools. Gayle Leach, a veteran school teacher, Sunday School teacher and child evangelist offers some thoughts on tools:

Using the right tool allows the teacher to make a functionally appropriate presentation of the Gospel.

I like my "toys". Costumes, musical instruments, puppets and other props and toys are more than what they appear to be. They are my "tools" and a means to an end. The "end" is the Good News being heard and understood by the hearer. The "end" is a decision to follow God and allow Jesus to be Lord.

A "tool" can be how you decorate the room where you meet. Consider simple decorations and a lack of clutter to minimize distractions. Careful, and sometimes unconventional, furniture arrangements will help you to make the most of your space.

Children (and parents) like to know what's next on the agenda during your meeting time. A picture schedule is a tool that can be better than just words and numbers on a sign. It will better communicate what's happening next. A picture for prayer time could be that of a praying child. Pictures for worship/song time might be worshipping/singing children. Activity time will show a picture of the planned activity. Story time can be shown with the picture of a book. Pictures of food items will depict snack time. Attach times to the schedule for yourself and all your helpers, and post your picture schedule for your group.

When choosing curriculum, be sure to pick one that can be adapted to your situation and classroom needs. Look for material that offers lots of choices.

Another tool is an Individual Spiritual Mentorship Plan. It will provide you with the information you need to better serve the student. It's a means to insure a safe and positive experience for the student and their family.

STRATEGIES FOR TEACHERS

- ☐ Learn as much as possible about your students and intellectual disability. You can make a BIG difference in the lives of students! Help them discover their areas of giftedness and encourage them to work on growth areas where they have potential for success.

- ☐ Go from the concrete to the abstract. Incorporate as many learning styles as possible: use object lessons and pictures, use music and songs, and play-acting to demonstrate the truth you are teaching. Use pass-around objects to help tactile and kinesthetic learners.

- ☐ Break concepts into bite-size easy to learn pieces.

- ☐ Give learners feedback immediately.

- ☐ Work together with the learner's parents and other ministry team members to put together an Individualized Spiritual

Mentorship Plan (ISMP). Regularly attend team meetings and write progress reports.

ESTABLISH POLICIES AND PROCEDURES THAT ACCOMMODATE DISABILITIES OF ALL TYPES

Establishing an ISMP for each student puts in place several policies and procedures, security, student relations, and other important topics. An integral part of the ISMP is the support team. The support team needs to include, but is not limited to, the names of parents, disability pastor, youth/children's pastor, Sunday school teacher, small group leader/teacher, and head pastor. Here are the procedures needed for putting together an ISMP.

1. Meet with the family and the student.

2. Make changes to the physical plant if needed.

3. Meet with the family, the student, and the support team.

4. Devise a plan that ensures a positive experience for the student and the family. Be certain to address the following issues: student/family information; service animal; communication issues (if non-verbal, what are the signals or signs given by the individual that indicate a need; language boards; sign language; amplification devices; easily understood); eating restrictions; physical needs; a "buddy"; an aid or nurse; Braille or large print; the color of print used in a power point presentation (not all color is easily seen); personal hygiene and whether or not help is needed (don't make the person wait and risk their embarrassment); and any other issues the family might want to have addressed.

5. Plan a time for a "meet and greet" with the student and new classmates. Everybody needs to ask their questions. If it is decided to not do this, state in the ISMP why or why not.

6. Keep these ISMP forms locked away due to privacy issues. We have this information so we can better minister to the individual, not so we can know stuff about the new people.

7. Schedule a Parent's Day once a quarter so they can see how their child is progressing.

8. List everything. Keep good records to protect yourself and the child.

In the appendices there are samples of three forms you will find useful in setting up your special needs programs. First is a student registration form, secondly is an ISMP form and third is an ISMP specifics record sheet that records dates and summaries of meetings.

Preserving and Respecting Fragility, Dignity, Individuality, Spirituality and Giftedness

This is a principle every educator and especially every Christian educator must live by. No matter what the student's chronological or cognitive age, these aspects of their personality must be recognized cherished and protected at all times and at all cost.

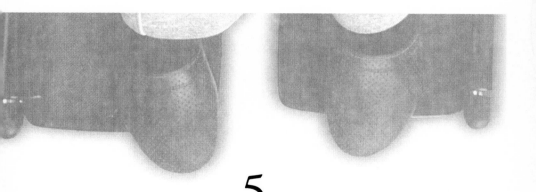

5.
Whosoever Will May Come: People with Moderate Intellectual Disabilities and the Worship Service

OBJECTIVES

- ☐ To know who you are trying to reach
- ☐ To understand your goal for each service
- ☐ To recognize the importance of tempo
- ☐ To focus on the need for simplified language
- ☐ To respect the ability of people with intellectual disabilities to interact with God
- ☐ To develop the need for sensitivity where appropriate touching is concerned
- ☐ To apply practical ideas for worship services designed for people with intellectual disabilities

THE CONCEPT

The implication of the Great Commission is that every person is entitled to the presentation of the gospel at their own level of understanding. By extension, a group of people with intellectual disabilities in a local church should be entitled to a worship service in which they can participate with full understanding.

Foundation Scripture

Mark 16:15
(The Great Commission)

INTRODUCTION

This chapter focuses on developing user-friendly worship services for people with low-functioning intellectual disabilities within a local church. Earlier, in chapter two, we discussed three approaches to including people with intellectual disabilities in the worship service. They were:

☐ Integrating people with intellectual disabilities into the general worship service. The advantage is that they are included in the gathering of the church family. The disadvantage is that they may have trouble understanding parts of the service.

☐ Having a separate service for people with intellectual disabilities. This approach has two distinct advantages. First, biblical truth is presented at a level the student can understand. Second, it allows for the creation of a dynamic, cohesive group of peers that can fellowship together, find ways to use their individual gifts, and bless the church family at-large. The major disadvantage is that this segregated group can become isolated from the larger church family to the point that it is virtually forgotten.

☐ A combined approach allows the group with intellectual disabilities to participate in the preliminary activities and general worship service, but at some point, they are dismissed to go to their own service in the same way that children are dismissed to go to children's church. It is nice to give the service for those with intellectual disabilities a name that distinguishes it from both the children's church and the youth group. For instance, at the appropriate time, one could announce, "It's now time to dismiss those who are involved in children's church, Rainbow Club, and Power Church." Rainbow Club and Power Church would distinguish your ministries to people with severe and profound intellectual disabilities and people with moderate intellectual disabilities from your children's church. This integrated approach allows people with disabilities to receive teaching at their level of understanding, bond with their peers and still be identified with the church family at-large.

KNOW WHO YOU ARE TRYING TO REACH

It is important to understand that ministry to people with low-functioning intellectual disabilities must be geared to their level. When they can understand and participate in it, everyone profits from the service.

LEARNING CHARACTERISTICS OF PEOPLE WITH LOW-FUNCTIONING INTELLECTUAL DISABILITIES

People with low-functioning intellectual disabilities are *real people* with the same basic needs all of us have. They need love, acceptance, and understanding to experience accomplishment. Because of sin, they need the message of the gospel. They can learn spiritual truths when taught on a concrete level and within their mental functioning range. *Learning takes place very, very slowly for people with low-functioning intellectual disabilities.*

- ☐ They cannot keep pace with their peers without disabilities because their response time is so much slower. Some pastors and worship leaders may not understand this because they see people with low-functioning intellectual disabilities dancing, clapping, and loving the fast, syncopated rhythms, beats, and the speed of modern worship songs. *They love the energy, but their minds can not process the information fast enough to participate in the worship.*

- ☐ They have short attention spans, and they cannot grasp abstract ideas well. Leaders must use concrete words, examples, and various types of audio-visual materials such as overhead projectors, slides, costumes, puppets, and drama to help them understand the message.

☐ Repeat simple truths over, and over, and over again, in many different ways.

☐ People with low-functioning intellectual disabilities do not have a normal curiosity to learn. Therefore, they are not motivated by normal internal and external motivators. However, they quickly form strong attachments to people, *so significant individuals in their immediate environment may become the chief motivational forces in their lives and in the learning process.*

UNDERSTAND YOUR GOAL FOR EACH SERVICE

Try to focus on one simple, single thought for the meeting. Review, re-emphasize, and re-tell that same thought in more than one way through songs, Scripture, stories, and preaching. Conclude with an altar call, asking for a response to God in the specific area that was addressed in the lesson.

Songs that seem to work best are songs which contain simple, concrete words they can understand and are no more than four lines in length. This eliminates many of the songs our churches sing because of their complicated words and abstract ideas. It also eliminates a lot of songs used in children's programs which are sung too fast, are syncopated, and have complex rhythms and too many verses.

SPIRITUAL CHARACTERISTICS OF PEOPLE WITH LOW-FUNCTIONING INTELLECTUAL DISABILITIES

People with low-functioning intellectual disabilities have the same spiritual needs that all of us have.

☐ They need the gospel.

☐ They can be aware of and can be taught the difference between right and wrong.

□ They will respond to the gospel when it is presented in a clear, simple message on their cognitive level. Remember, repetition is an important part of communicating spiritual truth.

□ *They have the same calling on their lives, the same gifts, and the same abilities everyone receives from God at birth. However, they do not have the opportunities to use or perfect their gifts and abilities. That is why disability ministry is so necessary.* It opens up opportunities for millions of God's children to display the grand and glorious gifts and talents that God has given these people who are ostracized from our society. The church is transformed as these gifts are allowed to be used. God teaches us tremendous truths about His love, acceptance, and accomplishments that come from humble obedience in situations in which God receives all the glory and honor.

Our goal is to bring them in as a caterpillar and release them as a butterfly.

The Importance of Tempo

Pacing and tempo are very important in ministering to people with low-functioning intellectual disabilities. In this context, pacing and tempo should be thought of as the speed at which a truth is being taught. When the service is geared simply enough, and the pace is slow enough for the participants to sing along with the songs, hear the question, be able to process it, and give an answer, then they are involved in the service. If the pace and vocabulary level gets fast and too complicated, students will lose interest, become distracted, and create disturbances. Look to see if they are mouthing the words to the song being sung. Check to see how many raise a hand with an answer to a question. *The goal is to get every person involved in the service and keep them involved from beginning to end.*

The key word in every aspect of ministry to people with low-functioning intellectual disabilities is SLOW, SLOW, SLOW. Move slowly, talk slowly, sing slowly, and transition slowly to keep pace with their response time and their ability to process information.

When a missionary goes into a new culture, he must immerse himself in order to learn the language, customs, dress, music, foods, and acceptable means of communication. His purpose is to find the most effective way to communicate the gospel to the people he is called to reach. We must use the same approach in disability ministry. Ask God to help you reach into the mind, thought processes, and lives of people with low-functioning intellectual disabilities to discover the keys to reaching them for Christ. We are looking for effective ministry that brings results.

THE NEED FOR SIMPLIFIED LANGUAGE

The language you use needs to be as simple as possible. Use concrete words to which your audience can relate. Abstract words carry no meaning for people with low-functioning intellectual disabilities. Therefore, a lot of adjectives that add color and descriptive detail to Bible stories only confuse them. They get lost in the extra words and miss the point of the story. As you study a Bible story, ask God to show you the main point. Ask yourself, "If I am not able to get anything else across, what is the one point God wants them to understand?" Then ask God to give you simple, concrete words to tell that story so they can understand it and even tell it back to you.

RESPECT THEIR ABILITY TO INTERACT WITH GOD

In some respects, people with low-functioning intellectual disabilities have a big advantage over those without intellectual impairment when it comes to connecting with God. Our lives have become so complex with schedules to maintain, bills to pay, success and failure issues, the many cares of this world, and the accumulation of earthly things. They have an advantage because:

- □ People with low-functioning intellectual disabilities live simple lives in thought, word and deed.

- □ They can give simple, undistracted attention to God and His Word.

- □ They have a simple faith that believes what the Bible says.

- □ They have a simple love for God.

- □ They forgive easily, love genuinely, and are often brutally honest.

We have so much to learn from them in spiritual issues. Working with people with intellectual disabilities is one of the greatest privileges God can give His children.

THE NEED FOR SENSITIVITY WHERE APPROPRIATE TOUCHING IS CONCERNED

Most people with low-functioning intellectual disabilities love affectionate hugs and touches. Because some have been disciplined for excessive hugging, we must be sensitive to each situation and take cues from the caregivers. It may be best to ask the caregiver if it is OK to hug the person with the disability. This is actually a very good protocol to adopt in any new situation. In our modern society, it is very important to be sensitive and respectful of the personal space of others.

PRACTICAL IDEAS FOR WORSHIP SERVICES DESIGNED FOR PEOPLE WITH LOW FUNCTIONING INTELLECTUAL DISABILITIES

Opening

Greet everyone and tell them simply what they can expect in the service. For instance you might say, "We will be singing songs. Many of you will play instruments in the orchestra; others will hold puppets and sing in the worship team. We will give testimonies and pray. We will have special music and a Bible story. Then we will ask God to help us obey His Word."

Orchestra

Many good rhythm band instruments such as sticks, shakers, bells, clappers, tambourines, drums, guitars, sandpaper blocks, etc. can be purchased. However, homemade ones work just as well. Do not use any instruments that are played with the mouth unless it belongs to a particular individual. It is not healthy to pass mouth instruments around in a service without sterilizing them after each person. In most situations, that is not practical, so it is best to eliminate mouth instruments. Old guitars are loved, even if they have only one string to pluck. Pass out instruments to those who would like to play in the orchestra, and have the musicians sit in their own chairs. The noise they produce may seem atrocious to human ears, but it is majestic and beautiful in God's ears. To watch them play with all their heart and sing at the top of their lungs is one of the most precious experiences this side of heaven.

Puppets

People with low-functioning intellectual disabilities often enjoy holding a puppet. Trying to move a puppet's mouth during the singing helps them feel important and gives them an additional way of participating in worship. If you are working with a large group, those who would like to use puppets could be invited to sit up in front of the others. In a small group, those operating the puppets would remain in their seats. A puppet curtain and/or stage are not necessary to successfully use puppets as aides in worship.

Worship Team

There are some in every group who always want to be up front, singing, helping to lead, and sometimes directing with their hands. Though they distract many with their antics, they always want to worship the Lord.

If microphones are available, use them even though it increases the volume of noise generated by the singing and orchestra. It may seem like total chaos, but if you listen with spiritual ears, you will hear the sound ascending to the Father with all its innocence, gusto, and passion like the sound of the most polished worship recording ever made. Hearts are moved to worship during this chaotic time. Most participants are giving everything they have. They are doing their best in singing, playing, and puppetry. This surely pleases God, for they are making a joyful noise before Him in worship just as He commanded us to do.

Songs

Friendship Club materials have many good songs that can be used. Here are some examples of simple, effective songs that use language that people with low-functioning intellectual disabilities can handle:

No One but Jesus

No one but Jesus makes bad people good. No one but Jesus, no one but Jesus. He is the Son of God."

Text and tune by Stella B. Daleburn © 1953, renewed 1981 Scripture Press Publications

My Best Friend is Jesus

My best friend is Jesus: Love Him, love Him. My best friend is Jesus: Love Him, love Him. Love Him."

You may insert other words for more verses

Text and tune by Mildred Adair Stagg from Songs We Sing © 1939. Renewal 1967 Broadman Press.

Other familiar tunes such as *The Farmer in the Dell* have new words such as:

"When you are afraid, and when you are alone, and when you don't know what to do, trust in the Lord."

Text by Florence Dieckmann, Roanoke, VA

To the tune of *Mary Had a Little Lamb*
I love God and He loves me......He's so good to me.
Do you know that God loves you.....You should love Him too.
Text by Ginger Cawthorne of Butler, PA.

Prayer

Many people with low-functioning intellectual disabilities love to pray. They are not self-consciousness about making mistakes or fumbling for words; they just express themselves purely and genuinely to God. That is true worship. They may need help with suggestions because many get caught up in thoughts about someone they know who is sick or has recently died. They need polite suggestions to help them pray for the needs of individuals in the service.

Testimonies

Since most churches never give people with low-functioning intellectual disabilities opportunities to testify, this is the place and the time for these children of God to give Him thanks and praise. Most testimonies are usually short and simple, consisting of one sentence. However, some individuals are very verbal and will preach a sermon. The leader might give them a hug when they stop to catch their breath and thank them for sharing that wonderful testimony. Be sure to tell them they can share again in another service or class.

Message

The simple point of the message should already have been targeted through the songs, prayers and other activities that have led up to this point in the service. The message should be a simple sharing of the story from God's Word emphasizing the one thing God wants them to understand. It can be told, and then retold using pictures, puppets, and drama. Have one participant come up and tell the story in his or her own words. Dress actors in costumes and help them act out the story. You may have to tell them every word to say and how to act, but the point is that they are dressed up and are saying the words and acting out the parts. This is their opportunity to use their God-given gifts to minister to their peer group.

Communion

Very few Christians with low-functioning intellectual disabilities have ever had communion. They don't know what it is or what it means.

Since they are able to know the Lord Jesus Christ as their personal Savior, they should also be able to receive communion. The centerpiece of the Kingdom ought to be the celebration of the King. Communion is an ordinance of the Church. It was instituted to regularly remind us of the price of our salvation. People with low-functioning intellectual disabilities need to be reminded of this and taught to celebrate the King as well. In many ways they are like children, irregardless of their chronological age. Jesus cautioned his disciples in Mark 10:1-16 not to under estimate their value.

> *Don't push these children away. Don't ever get between them and me. These children are at the very center of life in the kingdom. Mark this: unless you accept God's kingdom in the simplicity of a child, you'll never get in. Then gathering the children up in his arms, he laid his hands of blessing on them.* (The Message Bible)

There has been much discussion regarding the practice of serving communion to people with low-functioning intellectual disabilities, and there are many conflicting points of view. The following is the position endorsed by Special Touch Ministry.

The purpose of communion is symbolic. Communion reminds us that Jesus died on the cross for us, and that the Lord is coming back again to get us.

> *What you must solemnly realize is that every time you eat this bread and every time you drink this cup, you reenact in your words and actions the death of the Master...* (1 Cor. 11:26 Message Bible)

Those who work with people with low-functioning intellectual disabilities have the power to influence their lives for good or evil. We are responsible to lead them into godly experiences. Therefore, we should not hesitate to offer them salvation just as everyone else is offered salvation. We should not hesitate to offer them communion just as we offer it to everyone else who claims to be a Christian.

Personal preparation is necessary before one takes communion. That means an individual must confess his sin and receive Christ's forgiveness before he participates. Because it is very rare for individuals with low-functioning intellectual disabilities to be able to verbalize their faith, several questions are raised. How can they receive communion if they cannot verbalize their faith in God? How much do they understand, and how much are they just "parroting" their leaders? One can ask them, "Do you love Jesus?" and their reply may be, "Yes." "Do you want to live for Jesus?" "Yes." "Do you want to go to heaven when you die?" "Yes." How valid is this testimony?

While it's true we may not be able to determine how much they understand about salvation and communion because they cannot verbalize their thoughts, we are faced with the question, how many adults who can put their thoughts into words really understand it? How many of those same adults receive communion? What criteria do we use to judge these adults? We must let God be the judge. God is pleased when we offer His precious children the opportunity to celebrate communion and remember Him. Let's not get between them and Jesus because we have unanswered questions.

Some might ask, "What are the consequences if people with low-functioning intellectual disabilities take communion in an unworthy manner? Are we providing a way for them to sin against God?" In comparison with other people, individuals with low-functioning intellectual disabilities seem to be more willing and more comfortable in admitting their weaknesses and sins, confessing them immediately, and receiving forgiveness. They are not saddled with the pride and guilt that affect so many of us. God has given us the privilege and responsibility of leading people with low-functioning intellectual disabilities. It is not our job to judge them but to provide opportunities for them to follow God's Word in obedience with joy and gladness. The body of Christ needs to carry people with low-functioning intellectual disabilities along in the stream of God's mercy and grace.

Where do we believe children go when they die? To heaven? In the same way, a child (or a person with low-functioning intellectual disabilities) is fully accepted by God in death, they are fully accepted by God in life and are qualified to receive communion. Often they have greater faith in God than people without disabilities.

When serving communion to people with low-functioning intellectual disabilities, several things must be kept in mind when selecting the elements. Bread can be used, but it is crumbly when used for a large group, and breaking individual pieces off can be very difficult. Broken crackers will work, but they are irregular in size. The tiny wafers that can be bought for communion are often too small for their hands to handle, so dropping them becomes a problem. Experience has taught us that Oyster Crackers work well because they are uniform size and large enough for their hands to handle.

Though red grape juice or wine is often used for communion because it symbolizes Christ's blood, the colors and connections are not there for people with low-functioning intellectual disabilities. Also because their fine motor skills are often lacking, there is always a chance they will spill the juice on their clothes, the carpet, and/or on their caregivers. WHITE grape juice is a wise alternative because it does not stain. Three-ounce bathroom cups are also a good choice because they are much easier to handle than the small, standard-size communion cups. Put only enough juice in the cup to cover the bottom. This is equivalent to a small swallow. If you put more than that in a cup, they may slosh it on their face, dribble it onto their clothes, or choke on the volume. The amount of juice used is not an issue. The point of taking communion is to obediently remember Jesus' death on the cross. The less juice in the cup, the better it is for the ceremony.

When serving the elements, the leader should very simply explain the meaning of the cracker. He might say, "When our teeth crunch the cracker, it breaks up into pieces. That helps us think about how the body of Jesus was broken when He was nailed to the cross for our sins. The Bible also tells us that they beat Jesus with whips. Because that hurt, Jesus understands when our bodies hurt, and we can ask him to heal us when we are sick." Then have a member of the group thank Jesus for dying on the cross. Often these prayers can be a powerful experience for those listening.

The juice is a reminder of the blood of Jesus. His life blood washed away all our sins. A group member can express in prayer his or her simple thanks to Jesus for giving His blood to take away our sins. Allow the blessings of God to flow in waves of glory over your class and the service as you celebrate Jesus through communion.

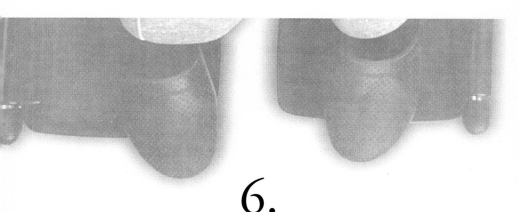

6.

"I Have a Disability?"
Understanding the Unique Needs
of People with Mild Intellectual
Disabilities

OBJECTIVES

- ☐ To understand the nature of mild intellectual disability

- ☐ To recognize the unique position this group holds within the community of people living with disabilities and understand the needs this position creates

- ☐ To understand the issues impacting this group.

- ☐ To develop strategies for communication, relationship building, and evangelism.

THE CONCEPT

Due to the nature of their impairment, most people with mild cognitive delay struggle to find a place of acceptance in society and in the community of people with disabilities. The heart of our message to them must be that when they find Jesus Christ, they have found their place. The church must be a reflection and extension of Christ's open heart and open arms.

Foundation Scripture

Ephesians 1:6 (KJV)
(The Church must not reject those whom
God accepts through Christ.)

WHAT IS "MILD INTELLECTUAL DISABILITY"?

From a layman's point of view, people with mild intellectual disabilities have a cognitive level ranging between approximately age twelve and higher. This is why communication, presentation, and teaching techniques commonly used with young people are effective with this group. However, there is a difference between using communication techniques that are effective with teenagers and treating adults in this people group as though they are teenagers. *They are not teenagers! They are adults with a teenage level of understanding. They face adult issues, and they deserve the same consideration due to adults.* The challenge for the pastor and Christian educator is to find ways to minister to their needs as adults and bridge the gaps created by their disabilities.

Although most of the people in this group have a teenage cognitive level, it is imperative to keep in mind at all times that they are not teenagers. They are adults and are completely worthy of the respect that adults deserve.

THE UNIQUE POSITION OF PEOPLE WITH MILD INTELLECTUAL DISABILITIES

People with mild intellectual disabilities have a unique position in the community of people with disabilities. The mild nature of their disability creates problems for them as they seek to find their comfort zone in society. Many people in this category can live essentially normal lives with a minimal level of assistance. Many finish high school, and some may even complete some level of post-secondary education. Some will live independently. They may marry and even own their own homes.

These achievements are often hard won. They come as a result of years of dedicated, hard work directed at overcoming their intellectual and social challenges. Unfortunately, their hard work is often rewarded by feelings of alienation. High-functioning individuals frequently feel like they don't fit among those with moderate and profound intellectual disabilities. In addition to their different intellectual levels, the groups have very different interests. They need different kinds of social interaction, and they have different personal concerns and goals. At the same time, those with mild intellectual disabilities often find they are not accepted by those with whom they work and interact in the "normal" world even though they usually hold jobs and live either semi-independently or completely on their own.

People with mild intellectual disabilities don't fit into an intolerant society's pre-conceived pigeonholes. This problem is most acutely felt by those with the highest levels of cognitive function. Because they are so close to the normal range of intelligence, they have a very difficult time confronting the reality that they have a disability that will create lifelong challenges and prevent them from being accepted in some circles. As a result, people in this group are often uncomfortable "in their own skin." They may try to cope with low self-esteem by refusing to recognize their limitations and denying their disability.

In the church world, programs for people with intellectual disabilities often make the mistake of lumping all participants together regardless of their mental level. This is unfair to those at both ends of the spectrum. Just as the church must recognize and meet the needs of people with severe and profound disabilities, it also needs to embrace those with mild intellectual disabilities and their unique needs.

WHAT ISSUES IMPACT THIS PEOPLE GROUP?

The critical issues that impact people with mild intellectual disabilities are some of the same issues every person confronts, regardless of whether or not they have a disability. They include building self-esteem, making healthy and holy lifestyle choices, and making and meeting life goals.

Building Self-esteem

Self-esteem is accepting and loving ourselves for who we are. It is recognizing that as a creation of God, we have inherent worth. God has designed each person with gifts and talents which can be used to fulfill their purpose in this world. However, we must also recognize that each of us has limitations, challenges and imperfections. The key to accepting the reality of these problems in our lives is realizing that God sees each of us exactly as we are, and He still loves us unconditionally. Self-esteem becomes an issue for those with mild intellectual disabilities when:

- Life experiences have broken their spirit.
- They fail to realize that they are of inestimable value no matter what their disabilities, limitations and challenges may be.
- They have been emotionally and spiritually brutalized by the process of formal or informal mainstreaming.
- They have never had a personal encounter with Jesus Christ.

When they are very close to the normal cognitive range, being confronted with the reality of their disability can create a self-esteem/self-image crisis because they don't consider themselves as being limited or different in their own minds. The following account illustrates the agonizing plight of those who are functioning at the highest cognitive level of intellectual disability. The name of this young man has been changed.

Josh

Josh was in his mid-twenties; he finished high school and is very bright. He lives at home and has attended a summer Christian camp/retreat program for people with disabilities for several years. Josh's intellectual disability is extremely mild. He strives and struggles to be accepted as a person without any intellectual limitations, but he is constantly frustrated in his attempts to achieve these goals. From his point of view, he only wants what most young men want in life: a good job, a girlfriend, a circle of friends with whom he can relate and who will appreciate him for who he is, and opportunities to fulfill God's plan for his life.

In his summer program, some of the guests at his intellectual level have been attending the chapel for people with physical disabilities because the chapel for people with intellectual disabilities is geared below their cognitive level. Josh has tried to make friends with and be accepted by those with physical disabilities, but for the most part he has alienated himself because of his tendency to force himself on others. Part of his disability is that he has difficulty determining which behaviors are appropriate to an occasion. Struggling with appropriateness is not uncommon for people with mild intellectual disabilities. Sometimes the intellectual disability of very high-functioning individuals manifests itself more as gaps in understanding rather than a lack of intelligence. Another manifestation may often be a lack of the emotional control. All of these factors conspire against Josh. The harder he tries, the more he inadvertently pushes people away from himself.

When he returned to camp the following summer, the organizers had decided to initiate a new morning chapel just for people with mild intellectual disabilities. The reason for starting the new program was not to isolate the high functioning, but to feed them spiritually at their own cognitive, emotional and social level, address their unique concerns, and provide social interaction and identification for those guests who share similar life situations and experiences.

When Josh tried to attend the chapel for people with physical disabilities, he was told he must attend the new program. His normally cheerful nature turned sullen and uncooperative. When the pastor conducting the chapel tried to talk to Josh at a later time, he was met with anger and resentment. Josh did not want to be grouped with those whom he considered to be mentally inferior. Over the next couple of years, Josh avoided coming to chapel at all, and eventually he quit attending the summer program altogether. Josh always resented being confronted with the reality of his own disability.

The story of Josh is tragic and poignant. Every one of us is on a life-quest. Every one of us is involved in a lifelong process of becoming. The tragedy of Josh's life is that in denying the reality of his challenges and limitations, he dedicated himself to trying to become someone he could never be.

Josh's perception of himself was based on several misconceptions. They included:

- "I don't have a disability that limits me mentally and socially."

- Intellectual disability makes a person inferior, un-cool and socially unacceptable.

- People without intellectual disabilities are to be envied.

- Fellowship with people with intellectual disabilities is undesirable and has nothing to offer.

Josh will continue to be stuck in an uncomfortable, solitary world. He is caught between that which he refuses to accept and those that refuse to accept him until he becomes comfortable in his own skin and makes the decision to love himself, warts and all.

Parenthetically, there are lessons to be learned from Josh's story for program directors, teachers and staff. When a new program is introduced for people with mild intellectual disabilities, it is very important that it be presented to the group of people involved in a positive and enthusiastic way. It should be presented as an opportunity and not a restriction or a punishment. The attitude they should hear in your voice is, "You *get* to participate in a new program!" This sounds much better than, "You *have* to participate in a new program!"

Healthy, Christ-centered self-esteem and self-acceptance is a key for anyone to become comfortable in their own skin. Achieving healthy self-esteem involves a three-step process: confronting limitations, connecting with the person and church of Jesus Christ, and finding a place in the body from which they can contribute.

Confronting Limitations

The first step toward healthy self-esteem for the intellectually challenged individual is to take ownership of their disability. The Tom Hanks film, *Forrest Gump*, is about a man who triumphs over the limitations of his intellectual disability by embracing them. He accepts himself for who he is and goes from there. In the movie, Forrest's mother, played by Sally Field, makes an important, although politically incorrect observation: "Stupid is as stupid does." In other words, an intellectual impairment is not the end of the world. It does not label a person as inferior nor does it mean they have nothing to offer.

Every person born in this world has challenges and limitations. Many of those challenges are even greater than living with disability. Life is a marathon, and not everyone starts from the front of the pack. None of us can change our starting place, but if we can confront our limitations honestly, we can minimize their impact on our outcome. Challenges and limitations cannot be dealt with and overcome until they are recognized. Limitations and impairments are overcome by understanding that we are more than the sum of our problems. We also have gifts, talents and abilities that God gave us to compensate for those challenges. People with mild intellectual disabilities have an intellectual impairment of one kind or another, but emphasizing that impairment is to look at the glass as half empty.

Connecting with the Person and Church of Jesus Christ

Just as the church must be accessible for people with physical disabilities, it must also be accessible for those with intellectual disabilities. An accessible church begins with accessible hearts that choose to live out the acceptance that Jesus Christ offers every person He died to save. The local church can do the following to connect with people with intellectual disabilities:

- Embrace them with acceptance and understanding.
- Help them find and develop their ministry gifts.
- Develop programs to meet their unique needs and tap into already existing programs offered by national ministries to people with disabilities.
- Develop opportunities for evangelism by establishing relationships with local group homes, workshop programs, and Special Olympics.

Intellectual disability can be uncomfortable to be around, but don't let the uneasiness that you and others in your church feel be misinterpreted as prejudice, unfriendliness, disinterest, or rejection. Don't let the following situations happen in your church:

Chuck

Chuck has been attending his neighborhood church for six months. He has repeatedly tried to be friendly, but he has found the people in the church to be standoffish and cliquish. He fully understands the impact his disability has on his life and on those around him. His only friend in the church was the associate pastor. When that pastor left the church, Chuck was left alone, and he eventually stopped attending.

Ronnie and Ellen

Ronnie and Ellen are two extremely high-functioning Christian young ladies. They completed high school, have jobs, and live semi-independently. They love their local church. They love worship and the ministry of the Word, yet they are ostracized by people in the church who are uncomfortable with the girls' mild intellectual disabilities. Although they have been in their church for many years, Ronnie and Ellen feel they are accepted by only a few individuals.

Fortunately Ronnie and Ellen found a refuge at the annual Special Touch Summer Get Away in Illinois. There they became the dynamic center of a lively group of guests with mild intellectual disabilities, and their core group has driven the growth of the larger group. Even though they meet only once a year, this segment of the Illinois program experienced a fourfold growth in nine years largely because the dynamic core group did not become a clique. They remained an open circle that joyfully accepted new members into the spiritual family they have created. The sad fact is that Ronnie and Ellen are forced to live on only four days of true Christian fellowship out of every 365. They, and others like them, need a church that will follow the model of being an "open circle" and a source of unconditional love and acceptance.

Tom

Tom is a highly intelligent, friendly, very well-groomed man in his late twenties or early thirties who has multiple intellectual disabilities. The compulsion caused by his autism has the side effect of making him good with numbers and categorizing items. He has had much success and personal fulfillment in his job at an auto parts store. In fact, he has found more acceptance working for NAPA than he has found in church.

The phobic responses to intellectual disability by Christians in the local church are costing the souls of precious people who Jesus Christ embraced in His death on the Cross. It is time to redeem these people and crucify the silly phobias.

When people with mild intellectual disabilities connect with Jesus Christ and a local church that loves and accepts them unconditionally, they are able to live out a new identity. They are no longer a person with an intellectual disability; they are a *Christian* with an intellectual disability. The presence and influence of Christ and His people in their lives makes a vital difference and enables them to fulfill their God-given potential.

Contributing to the Fulfillment of the Great Commission

Every Christian, regardless of their challenges in life, has a place of ministry in the body of Christ. From there, they can contribute to the ministry of the local church and fulfill the Great Commission (1 Cor.12; Eph. 4). People with mild intellectual disabilities often have the energy and desire to grow in Christ and make a difference in the world. They only need a pastor and a church body with the wisdom and compassion to see their potential and give them proper training and opportunities for service.

Making Healthy and Holy Lifestyle Choices

All human beings have to deal with issues regarding their sexuality, and adults and adolescents with mild intellectual disabilities are no exception. Intellectual delays sometimes impair the capacity of individuals to make sound choices.

Although the local church may not like it, they must deal with this subject because the church is the only force and voice for righteousness in the world. The church must use that voice to guide and instruct people with intellectual disabilities in these personal areas because they are being bombarded on every side by other voices that are telling them to indulge themselves however they see fit. These other voices carry great influence; they are the voices of educators, doctors, house parents, and social workers. Biblically based teaching needs to be given on the subjects of self-control, self-respect, respect for others and moral accountability for choices and decisions.

Making and Meeting Life Goals

Many people with mild intellectual disabilities become frustrated because it is difficult to meet their life goals and make their dreams come true. The social service system often sets minimal life goals for their clients. These basic goals usually include the completion of secondary education and finding a job. After the school requirements are met, Social Services stamps their case file "Complete" and moves on. However, there is much more to life than completing high school and finding a job. People with mild intellectual disabilities have dreams like everyone else. They often dream of marriage and a family, a home of their own, and a career that goes beyond just having a job.

The local church cannot always facilitate all of these dreams, but it can be a source of inspiration and encouragement. It can strive to make sure individuals do not give up and let their dreams die of neglect.

COMMUNICATION, RELATIONSHIP BUILDING, AND EVANGELISM

People with mild intellectual disabilities enjoy connections and friendships. They need friends who, though not impacted by disability, will accept them as equals. Having a close friend in the so-called "normal" world helps them to understand the unconditional love of God. This can also help bridge gaps in their understanding and assist them in navigating through the social minefield of non-disabled society.

They also need opportunities to bond with people in their own situation. Building a strong support group of people with mild intellectual disabilities within the church creates a self-sustaining vehicle for building self-esteem, facilitating fellowship and fostering spiritual growth. Generally speaking, those in this group love activity and opportunities for interaction like bowling, roller skating, swimming and game nights. The church can use activities like this to build relationships and Christian fellowship.

Those who work with this group need to create an environment of unconditional acceptance and communicate to each individual that they are loved and valued by God, their friends, and their church family. Every participant should feel like they have finally found their place at the "cool kids' table."

Christians with mild intellectual disabilities love God and have a deep desire to grow spiritually. When they find a church where they feel accepted and loved, they can be a faithful and enthusiastic part of the church family. They love high-energy worship, ministry from the Word on their level that is relevant to their lives, and opportunities for spirit-to-spirit interaction with God around the altar.

Experience has proven that using methods similar to those used in teaching and presenting the gospel to teenagers can be equally effective with people who have intellectual disabilities. The acronym **FIRE** can be used to describe this approach.

Focus

Focus on one concept or idea at a time. Don't create confusion by presenting too many concepts at one time. Although you may deal with different aspects of a subject in a service, deal with only one subject per service.

It is a good idea to frame the idea you are trying to communicate in one concise, easy to understand sentence. One experienced teacher and evangelist calls this "the bubblegum thought," because the main idea of message is captured in one sentence that the participants can "chew on all day." Tie the bubblegum thought to a supporting scripture verse, and anchor both with concrete illustrations on a chalkboard, whiteboard, easel or screen. The bubblegum thought should be introduced with an object lesson and supported by a Bible story that can be presented in a number of ways. One of the most effective ways to get the message across is to have participants from the audience or congregation spontaneously act out the story.

When teaching an abstract concept, go from the concrete to the abstract. For instance, when teaching on aspects of the love of God, one teacher used a mother's hug to illustrate her point. Remember; keep the focus on one concept.

Involvement

Identifying and connecting with your congregation of people with mild intellectual disabilities is crucial to communicating the gospel to them from the pulpit. They must never feel that you are speaking down to them. Get them personally involved in both the service as a whole and the presentation of the gospel from the platform.

People with mild intellectual disabilities can perform almost any role in a service. They can usher, sing in the choir, make announcements, play in the band, participate in a drama, run an overhead projector and/ or preach depending on their cognitive level and areas of giftedness. One of the greatest challenges people in this group face is that others in the church have a tendency to underestimate their ability and potential. Giving them opportunities to be involved in church services can encourage people and give them the affirmation they need to pursue God's larger plan for their lives.

Spontaneously acting out Bible stories or illustrating concepts is an exciting way to involve your entire congregation in your presentation. While costumes and props can be used, they are not necessary. Due to the nature of the disability involved, scripts should absolutely NOT be used. The minister or facilitator on the platform acts as a coach or prompter throwing the actors their lines. Professionalism is in no way required and is not the purpose of the exercise. The purpose of the exercise is to communicate the reality of the love of God and to use people with intellectual disabilities in communicating the reality of the love of God.

Christian educators, ministers, staff members, parents and care providers should never underestimate the capacity of a person with a disability to participate in such an exercise if that person is willing to participate. Sometimes participants with a lower cognitive ability will find their way into the service and want to be involved. Go with the flow and anointing of the Spirit and never discourage their attempt to step out of their world into a larger place.

Recognize that in every congregation there are both introverts and extroverts. The extroverts can often dominate and displace those who are introverted because extroverts are ready, willing and able to roll over them in their enthusiasm to participate. The solution is to prepare for the participation of both types of people ahead of time. Those with outgoing personalities will eagerly volunteer for larger speaking roles. Folks who are a little more timid may take smaller parts or act as "spear carriers" or silent "living props." The majority, who will remain in their seats, can still be very vocal participants. The idea is to encourage 100% participation from the crowd. Involvement in what is being taught creates internalization. When people internalize the truth that is being communicated they are able to make quality decisions that result in lasting change.

Reiteration

In a traditional sermon a main point is presented and then undergirded by supporting points. In a presentation to people with mild intellectual disabilities, the main point or bubblegum thought is taught and then taught again from a slightly different point of view or reinforced using a different method. For example, the bubblegum thought may be presented visually and verbally and then illustrated using a skit and then presented in the form of teaching the congregation a chorus or song that expresses the same truth. (Incidentally, choruses and songs are excellent ways of internalizing spiritual concepts.)

Reiteration is necessary for people with intellectual disabilities in order to accommodate the problems associated with cognitive delay. People learn in different ways because they have different learning styles. Their learning orientation may be visual, auditory, or tactile which means they learn best through what they see, what they hear, or what they touch. Therefore reiteration should incorporate all three of these learning styles. Audiovisual presentations can enhance a simply verbal presentation of the gospel. Object lessons can further aid those who have a tactile learning orientation.

Energy

Energy and excitement are crucial to a service for people with intellectual disabilities. Energy captures attention and fosters involvement. Because people with intellectual disabilities are prone to have short attention spans, it is important to have energy shifts during the service. Shift energy through changes in tone and in the manner of your presentation. While you want to present, reiterate and reinforce *one* main idea, you want to *vary* the way that concept is presented. Never allow the energy in a service to lag or become static. Never spend too much time on any one part of the order of service.

For instance, if you are presenting a Bible verse for memorization use several different methods of repetition to get your participants to assimilate the verse. Use high energy. Divide the congregation into sections and have them compete to see which section can repeat the verse loudest and with the greatest accuracy. There are many other assimilation methods you may use, but on rare occasions NONE of them may work. Sometimes there are outside factors that may impact the ability of people with mild intellectual disabilities to assimilate concepts. This is especially true in a camp, retreat or other recreational environment where participants may be involved in other high-energy activities prior to the chapel period. In these settings, fatigue can become a major factor.

When this occurs, do not keep trying to push them to respond to some pre-determined expectations you may have developed in your own mind. Move on to the next part of the program and change the energy to allow the congregation to refocus. Facilitating opportunities to refocus is key because refocusing re-energizes attention span. Capturing and maintaining attention is essential for internalization and internalization is essential for lasting spiritual results.

Moving the program along and changing energy frequently is important because it allows the congregation to refocus. Refocusing re-energizes their attention span.

The Bottom Line

Abe Goldstein is the son of missionary parents in West Virginia. He has a mild intellectual disability, but he is following his dream and pursuing God's call on his life to preach the gospel. He is in the process of completing courses required for ministerial credentials and has already had a tremendous impact as a preacher, missionary, and a minister of helps. Abe preaches, plays drums, does skits and drama, and is an indispensable help to his parents who direct a residential ministry for people with disabilities. At any given time, Abe can be found helping people in wheelchairs, driving them to and from the swimming pool or other activities, assisting with sound, preparing the platform for ministry, and helping in a hundred other ways. Abe has succeeded against the odds because his parents instilled in him energy, determination and the conviction that the God who called him into ministry is bigger than his limitations.

Abe is a prime example of what is possible when an individual has the proper encouragement, a positive environment, and people who were willing to look beyond the life challenges and disabilities and give him or her opportunities to develop and use their gifts to fulfill God's plan for their life.

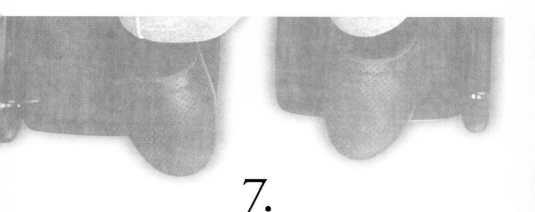

7.

Inside the Prison of Physical Disability

OBJECTIVES

- ☐ To begin to develop an understanding of the mindset of people impacted by physical disability.

- ☐ To begin to develop an understanding of the world of physical disability and the "bars" that constitute their "prison."

- ☐ To begin to develop strategies for communication, relationship building, and evangelism with people who have physical disabilities.

THE CONCEPT

The limitations and confinement of physical disability create a prison-like environment that is inherently discouraging due to the specific aspects of disability. Living in this atmosphere may cause individuals to doubt deeply held core beliefs and to surrender to their circumstances rather than pursue the good plan that God still has for their lives.

Foundation Scriptures

Matt. 11:2 (Prison made John the Baptist reevaluate his core beliefs)
Jeremiah 29:11 (God has a plan for every individual's life.)

INTRODUCTION

Each one of us has experienced trauma and tragedy. Those experiences go by many names: divorce, cancer, the loss of a child, a car accident, or the suicide of a loved one. Many times these kinds of tragedies can be life shattering. Life shattering experiences may disconnect us from everything and everyone we know and love. Life becomes a collection of fragments. We can become disconnected from our work, our play, our dreams and desires, our friends and family, and even our faith in God. This chapter examines the mindset and circumstances of individuals who have experienced trauma that results in a long-term physical disability.

It is important to understand at the outset that individuals with disabilities are just that - individuals. Not everyone enters the world of disability in the same way, and no one perceives or experiences that world in exactly the same way. Some people are born with a disability, while others lose health and wholeness suddenly and unexpectedly. Still others, such as those with multiple sclerosis or Parkinson's disease, lose their health in slow agony. Those born with a disability are generally better adjusted to their situation than those who experience disability as a result of a trauma such as an unexpected illness like a stroke, or a sudden accident. Accidents run the gamut from the commonplace such as diving into shallow water or being involved in a car wreck or motorcycle accident, to the uncommon and bizarre. Those in this later, "strange but true," category include a person who became a quadriplegic as a result of a tug-of-war game at college, and an individual who became a quadriplegic after being shot by an assailant from the seat of a motorcycle. Another lost both arms because of burns he sustained when he was hit with 13,000 volts of electricity high above the ground in a work-related accident. While God preserved his life from multiple system failures, he still lost his arms.

Because every person is different, some of this material may be rather general. While it may be most relevant to those who enter the world of disability suddenly and unexpectedly, most people with physical disabilities will have this "prison experience" to one degree or another.

Is this prison real?

While physical disability is literally physically confining, it also creates a prison in a mental, emotional, and spiritual sense. When some people read that last statement they scoff. They say things like, "I thought you were going to talk about a *real* prison! This is just psychobabble! It's a lot of soft, emotional coddling for people that just need to get real and pull themselves up by their own bootstraps! Life isn't all sunshine and Spam for anybody!" Dr. Dayton Kingsriter once told a class of future pastors that they could ignore psychological and sociological factors in people and churches if they wanted to, but that did not make those factors any less real. They would still have to be dealt with.

Prison bars don't have to be literally visible to surround someone; they don't have to be literally felt to be impregnable. That should be evident by the number of people in our society who must take medication for depression and other similar conditions. John the Baptist was put into a real prison but it affected him psychologically, emotionally, and spiritually. The darkness, the disconnection from his life and ministry, and the isolation took their toll on him to the point that he doubted the core beliefs that made him who he was. At his lowest point, he began to doubt that Jesus was the Christ (Matt. 11:20).

The Mindset of People with Physical Disabilities

This biblical episode encapsulates the reality of a prison created by disability. There are three elements involved in building this prison. (1) There is a sense of overwhelming helplessness when all control has been lost. (2) There is the feeling of being disconnected from everything and everyone in life. (3) There is perception that life has been shattered beyond repair. For Christians and even nominal believers in God, there is a fourth factor. It is hard to accurately name or define, but there is a sense of betrayal. Let's examine each of these elements individually.

There is a sense of being overwhelmed. If someone threw a brick at you, you might be injured, but you would probably recover rather quickly. However, if a dump truck dumped a full load of bricks on your unsuspecting body, recovery might not be so certain. Disability, like many other kinds of trauma, is similar to being buried under a truckload of bricks. Take the example of a quadriplegic. When the doctor comes in and tells his patient that he will never walk again, he's giving him the good news. The doctor is saving the worst for future visits in which he will describe the delights of this particular brand of disability. "The rest of the story" as Paul Harvey would say, includes chronic phantom pain, the inability to bear children, sexual complications, chronic urinary infections, urinary incontinence, involuntary bowel movements, and many, many more complications. Remember, this list reflects *only* the medical problems. Right away, you can see that each item on that list is a crisis in itself. Taken together along with social, financial, emotional, and other factors, it is easy to grasp the overwhelming nature of disability and understand how the total inability to cope can send people into a dark world of depression and despondency.

There is a sense of being disconnected from everything and everyone in life. Disability is a bully. It wants to dominate and overshadow every other thing in a person's life. This is especially true in the beginning during the trauma stage. The new victim of disability finds himself ripped away from his past life. His daily routine no longer consists of going to school or to work; it now revolves around doctors, nurses, therapists, psychiatrists, their various demands, and whether to have the green or the red Jell-O for lunch.

The sense of disconnection extends to relationships because, for at least a while, learning to cope with the new and scary world of disability and all of its ramifications becomes a full-time job. While most people in the life of someone new to disability can leave the hospital room, think about other things, and return home to their normal routine, the person overtaken by disability does not have those luxuries.

Disability becomes a 24-hour companion/nightmare, and it may take a long time for individual to gain enough perspective to be able to define themselves by anything other than their disability.

An unfortunate byproduct of this self-absorption is that relationships can begin to fragment and fall apart. Friends become alienated from the person with the disability because he seems concerned with only his situation and that which directly affects him. Statistics reveal it takes from one to five years for a person to completely integrate their disability into their life and accept both its blessings and curses. This sense of disconnection and isolation also explains why divorce and suicide rates for people with disabilities are significantly higher than for the general population.

There is a perception that life has been shattered beyond repair. This comes from being ripped away from a sense of normalcy and everything that was fun and familiar. The sooner a person with a disability begins to have fun, recognizes that the sun still rises in the morning, the birds still sing in the springtime, and McDonald's still makes pretty good cheeseburgers, the sooner the sense of irreparable damage will begin to dissipate.

There is a disconnection from belief or trust in God. This is a complex issue, and it manifests itself differently in believers and non-believers. In this context, the term "believers" is being used in the broadest possible sense. The reason calamity shakes faith is because, regardless of our religion or denomination, each person holds a secret tenet of faith in the depths of their heart. Logical or not, it is framed something like this, "Because I love God, and He loves me, God won't allow anything really, really bad to happen to me." We see evidence of this belief in the books people write about why bad things happen to good people. When people experience a profound personal tragedy, they often feel that a serious injustice has been done to them.

For unbelievers, disability confirms their conviction that the sky above is empty, and it fuels the anger that often feeds unbelief. Unbelief is sometimes the result of outrage over the fact that God permits loss.

This incredibly complex issue can be summarized in one question. Resolving this one question becomes the goal of disability ministry. The question is this, "God, if You are real, if You are really all-powerful and all-loving, if You have a good

plan for my life, and if You are at work in my life, how could You allow this terrible thing to happen to me?"

RESOLVING THE QUESTION

It is important to note that the goal of disability ministry is to *resolve* this question and not to provide answers or reasons for why God allows disability or other tragedies to come into the lives of His people. Victims of calamity may never know the reasons for their tragedies this side of Heaven, but the question is resolved when they are reconnected with God. Reconnection often happens when victims of tragedy experience the touch of God's unconditional love through the Christians around them. Unconditional love reveals God's unceasing care in spite of catastrophe or disaster. Unconditional love rekindles faith and gives those with questions the hope and patience they need to wait for the answers.

This truth can be examined through a Bible study based on the book of Ruth. After the catastrophic loss of her husband and sons, Naomi was left bitter, destitute, and feeling abandoned by God. Her faith was restored through Ruth's unconditional love. Ruth, in turn, was brought to God through the unconditional love of Boaz. It is important to note that while their heart aches were healed, it is unclear if their questions were ever answered in this life.

In the following examination of the prison bars created by disability, suggestions for the practical application of unconditional love are given at the end of each section. These suggestions will help you develop strategies for communication, relationship building, and evangelism. As you minister to people with physical disabilities and help them to break through their prison bars, don't rest in the power of these suggestions or in the cleverness of your strategies. Rather, seek the anointing God gives to set captives free.

If the Church is going to show unconditional love to people with disabilities, it must enter into their world and into their humiliation by becoming the eyes of Christ, the voice of Christ, the hands of Christ, the smile of Christ, and the heart of Christ. Prejudgment or condemnation will only alienate and close doors to future opportunities.

UNDERSTANDING THE "BARS" THAT CONSTITUTE THE PRISON

Illusion

The illusion of disability is twofold. First of all, disability is a bully. It comes into a life and grabs its victim by the throat. It dominates and overshadows every area of life. Tragedies such as disability change perception. Where once there was a rainbow, now there are only shades of gray. Because it is difficult to compartmentalize, the victim can lose the capacity to put their disability in perspective. For example, many people came to admire the focus and determination Christopher Reeve brought to his quest to regain his ability to walk. However, sometimes in their determination to regain what was lost, a person begins to equate walking again with happiness and fulfillment. Their heart's cry is, "If only I can walk again, then the rainbow will come back!" The ultimate need of every soul to find redemption, peace, and wholeness through Jesus Christ can be obscured by the domineering bully of disability.

Because the prison of disability is so dark, God seems distant and uncaring. Make no mistake, the Bible is crystal clear on this point. There is nothing you can do, no mistake you can make, no depth of personal failure you can reach, and no calamity that can overtake you that will ever change the fact that the Almighty God who created this entire universe, loves you absolutely, totally and completely forever. He is personally and absolutely committed to your eternal well-being. (John 3:16; Romans 8:35-39).

What You Can Do to Combat the Illusion

The overbearing bully of disability can be brought to its knees through the development of perspective. When a person with a disability develops the proper perspective, he or she views their disability realistically and understands that disability is not the worst thing that can happen to a person. A person with a disability needs friends who will speak truth and remind them that disability, like most unfortunate circumstances, is not all bad. A healthy perspective is reflected in the following wry observation made by a single young man who lived life in a wheelchair. "There are at least three good things about my disability: I get great seats at concerts, single girls love the wheelchair, and it's not cancer." Usually this is a message that people who are new to the community of people with disabilities have to hear from another person in that community. This fact underscores the value of Christian support groups and recreational programs for people with disabilities.

However, friends without disabilities can also be effective in helping an individual gain perspective. It is essential that a person with a disability understands that the challenges others face in life can be just as devastating and difficult as living with a disability. A key point that can dramatically change one's perspective is that a believer is *not a person with a disability*; he or she is a *Christian with a disability*. Too often Christians are guilty of identifying and defining themselves by their weaknesses and limitations instead of the power and potential provided by Jesus Christ (Phil. 4:13).

Regarding the bully represented by his Parkinson's disease, Michael J. Fox once said, "I can give it all of the space it needs, but I cannot give it all of the space it wants."

Impropriety

The chameleon-like ability to blend into a crowd and become anonymous is a luxury people with disabilities do not have. Impropriety is a constant issue, and it is characterized by embarrassing and humiliating incidents.

Joni Earickson Tada was at a Christian conference when impropriety reared its ugly head. She was seated in the back row of an auditorium that had an angled floor. When her caregiver emptied Joni's leg bag, she forgot to replace the cap. While her caregiver was away, a man in the row ahead noticed a yellow trickle flowing downhill on the floor in front of him. He turned to Joni and said, "Miss, I think you have a problem."

Rev. Tom Leach, a minister who is a quadriplegic, has also had his share of misadventures including flipping his wheelchair over in a restaurant doorway, and getting caught in elevator doors. On his first day as a high school teacher, the temperature rose into the 90s. Whenever the temperature is extremely hot or cold, Tom's legs tend to have violent muscle spasms. Just before the dismissal bell rang for the day, it was very quiet in a study hall. Suddenly, Tom's leg shot out, and his shoe flew off, hitting an unsuspecting girl, who was dozing off, in the head. Needless to say, she never fell asleep in class again.

Another classic example is given by Dave Roever who was severely burned during the Vietnam War. The reconstructive plastic surgery on his face was done in various stages. One day when he was en route to the hospital, Dave stopped for a traffic light. When the driver in the next car looked over at Dave, he was so startled that he drove his car through the wall of a Dairy Queen.

Sometimes impropriety is a necessity. For example, when a person with no arms goes out to a restaurant, he must either ask a dinner companion to feed him, or he must put his face down to his food. Someone with a full leg bag may have to ask a stranger to empty it for him or risk wetting his pants. A nonverbal person must prevail upon people to use a talk board to communicate with him or remain imprisoned by isolation. When a building is inaccessible to a person in a wheelchair, he must risk humiliation and injury by being carried up the necessary flights of stairs.

The only refuge and defense a person with a disability has in these circumstances is a good sense of humor. As one quadriplegic said, "Every day is a trip to Disney World when you live in a wheelchair; you never know what kind of ride the day will bring."

What You Can Do to Diminish the Sense of Impropriety

The value of a healthy sense of humor cannot be underestimated. One of Satan's greatest weapons in breaking the spirit of any person who experiences devastating tragedy is to get them to wallow in self-pity. A self-deprecating sense of humor that attempts to find the lighter side of disability and its accompanying incidents of impropriety can help break the backs of the twin serpents of self-pity and self-absorption. Friends must help a person with a disability learn to accommodate and facilitate the development of a sense of humor. Often the healthiest way for a person to remove the prison bar of impropriety is to poke fun at his own disability. The emotional release this creates promotes mental, emotional and spiritual health and does miracles in the process of adjusting to life with a disability. Humor releases endorphins which are natural healing chemical agents that fight depression and mental illness.

This can be a sensitive area because our society has taken political correctness to an extreme. It is sometimes difficult for friends and family to adjust to the fact that people impacted by physical disability often take tremendous delight in being politically incorrect. They make jokes about themselves and their conditions that would be considered insensitive and rude in polite society. Bystanders can be shocked and appalled when overhearing people with disabilities refer to themselves as "gimps" and "crips." Is this kind of behavior justifiable or excusable? Perhaps not, but it is understandable. Members of the community of people with disabilities consider their politically incorrect, self-deprecating humor a privilege of membership.

There is also another aspect of humor that should also be examined. Carman, the contemporary Christian musical artist and evangelist has observed that mocking the enemy helps to deprive him of his power to control your life. Although Carman was referring to how he treats Satan in his songs, the principle applies to life with a disability. *In learning to laugh at his or her situation, a person with a disability breaks out of a victim mentality and removes the fangs of the serpent that infect the soul with self-pity and self-absorption. Self-deprecating, politically incorrect humor can detoxify the human spirit because the power of the disability to dominate one's life is diminished when one takes the initiative and moves outside of accepted boundaries.*

Mocking Goliath whittles him down to size.

Indignity

Modesty and dignity are often the first two casualties of disability. Medical and practical necessities require that dignity and modesty be sacrificed in order to meet the needs of an injured person so he may live. Unfortunately, those in the medical profession who perform vital emergency services can be perceived as cold and methodical. The reality is that in such a situation, compassion is measured by speed, efficiency, and competence. In a crisis, there is no time for niceties or warm fuzzies.

Imagine how you would feel if the sanctity of your privacy was violated not just one day, but every day for the rest of your life in order to accomplish the daily necessities of getting dressed, going to the bathroom, and taking a shower. These procedures are every bit as invasive, intrusive, and embarrassing as you think they might be. They also enhance feelings of helplessness and worthlessness.

The realities of the modern health-care profession make this situation even worse. Home health aides get paid very little and are often overworked. This creates a high staff turnover for companies that place them and has a negative impact on their clients and their families who must endure a steady stream of semi-competent health aides with varying degrees of dedication. Often the new aide is there just long enough to learn the client's routine, and then they are out the revolving door only to be replaced by another rookie. Most of these people are not career health professionals. Many just answering an ad in the paper and have no idea what the job entails. They often quit after they realize why they have to wear gloves. In the period of one year, one client had as aides a part-time pig farmer, a woodcutter, a lady wrestler, a girl who was into the Goth sub-culture which borders on witchcraft and Satanism at times, and the wife of an Elvis impersonator, among others. Diversity is no crime, and almost anyone can be trained to be a personal care provider, but the really good ones are motivated, dedicated, and committed to providing compassionate care. When a client is blessed to have a dedicated health-care professional, one of two things usually happen. Either the company burns them out by overworking them, or the job becomes a steppingstone to nursing school or other advanced training.

The cumulative effect of this sometimes comical and colorful parade isn't funny. When home health-care works best, the health aide becomes a trusted and beloved member of an extended family. One nurse even compared it to the marriage relationship because it involves a level of intimacy and commitment. The person with a disability and the health aide are partners working together toward a common goal. At its very worst, the continual parade of people coming through the revolving door sends the message that the daily invasion, intrusion and violation of human dignity mean nothing because the person with the disability doesn't need care and respect; they are "just another piece of meat."

What You Can Do about Indignity

A local church might set up a respite ministry that could help provide personal care for people with disabilities and relieve regular family caregivers. The biggest misconception about providing care for people with physical disabilities is that it takes a "special person." Ministries such as Special Touch Ministry, Inc. have proven that homemakers, teachers, truck drivers, computer programmers, and almost anyone else with a compassionate heart, willing hands, and the ability to follow instructions can learn to provide personal care.

If you are caring for the personal needs of a person with a disability, or are present when such needs are being addressed, always treat the person with the highest measure of respect. As a practical matter, help maintain a degree of modesty and dignity by keeping the individual's body covered as much as possible. Keep in mind that their visual perspective may not allow them to always see when they are exposed. You can also contribute to the preservation of the dignity by helping them maintain the highest possible standards of personal hygiene.

Jesus Christ demonstrated that true ministry is "washing feet." Washing the feet of others is to enter into their humiliation willingly and without pre-judgment. It is to identify with their weaknesses and limitations without stripping them of their dignity. It is to minister to the necessities those weaknesses create while removing them as a barrier to fellowship and understanding. It is coming down without putting down. It is using what songwriter Michael Card referred to as, "the warmth of the water and tenderness of the towel" to cleanse, refresh, renew, and restore. Using this model any church or group of believers can restore dignity, not only to people with disabilities but all who are disenfranchised.

Remember Jesus washed the feet of his disciples to show He identified with their weaknesses and limitations, but in doing so, He did not strip them of their dignity. Personal physical care cleanses, refreshes, renews, and restores the spirit and emotions as well as the physical body.

Immobility

The lack of mobility is another of the inescapable core issues facing a person with a disability. Mobility consists of two elements, the ability to move about independently, and the ability to initiate and carry out a plan of action. Mobility is freedom to do what we want, when we want to do it. Living with disability often means that one's participation in life becomes dependent on the cooperation of others. The person with disability must contend with their caregivers' personal needs, agendas, and shortcomings. If the caregiver is a relative, such as a husband, wife, or parent, the situation becomes even more complicated. Rarely do people with a disability enjoy being a taskmaster. On the other hand, they need someone to become an extension of their own body; they require someone to be their hands and feet. Their power to initiate a plan of action has been stripped away. Imagine being unable to take a shower or turn the pages of a book without help. Imagine what it would be like to always need a "middleman" to meet your daily needs, achieve your goals, and fulfill your dreams

The bitter reality is that people with a confining physical disability are the same as everyone else in their heart and soul. Each has desires and dreams they would like to see fulfilled, but they are independent spirits trapped in dependent bodies. A person does not realize how much independence contributes to self-worth and the overall feeling of well-being until it is stripped away.

The bitter reality is that a person with impaired mobility is an independent spirit trapped in a dependent body.

The problem with needing a middleman is that too often the person with a disability is forced to live at the mercy or convenience of the caregiver. Imagine the frustration of waiting for an important phone call, and when the phone rings, you aren't able to answer it even though it is only six inches away. Your frustration multiplies when your caregiver refuses to answer the phone because he or she is otherwise disposed.

Suppose you are in the middle of teaching an 11th grade world history class when "the plumbing" that helps you to urinate completely and unobtrusively suddenly disconnects because your caregiver was distracted that morning and didn't do his or her job carefully. As a result, you wet your pants and embarrass yourself in front of a roomful of teenagers.

Now think about going to the mall. You see a CD that you have been looking for in the music store, and you want to stop and pick it up, but before you can say anything, the person pushing your wheelchair has spotted something they have been looking for in a store five doors down on the right. Before you know it, you are at an import store looking at African kitchen essentials.

These incidents may seem petty or nitpicky, but for a person with a disability, these kinds of events are not isolated occurrences; they are a daily challenge. From the caregiver's perspective, it must be said that a person has only two hands, and needs and tasks have to be prioritized. That is the dilemma in this issue. There is a legitimate need for prioritization, and waiting becomes a routine part of daily life for a person with a disability - but that doesn't make it easier. The person with the disability has three options. He can completely surrender his independence and let others make every decision for him. He can go to the opposite extreme and become a controller and manipulator by taking advantage of his disability and learning to pull strings and push buttons. The third and most difficult option is to learn to negotiate and communicate.

What You Can Do to Lessen the Pain of Immobility

When you or members of your ministry team encounter someone with a disability, you need to evaluate that person's needs. This does not have to be a formal evaluation, it can simply be done through observation. Ask yourself, "What does this person need in order to get around better in their home and in our community?" Here is a list of some of the things that they might need:

- ☐ A wheelchair, a ceiling mounted track system, a walker, or cane

- ☐ An intercom or other communications device – very inexpensive in today's world

- ☐ A computer – which does not have to be new or the top-of-the-line.

- ☐ Reaching devices and turntables or Lazy Susans to help them access items on tables or desks

- ☐ Ramps

An occupational therapy consultant can help you develop a more detailed list. Proper equipment for the home is only the beginning. They may need transportation to church, the market, or the doctor's office. If a church has a bus ministry, the bus could be used one day during the week to transport senior citizens and people with disabilities to the market. With some imagination and a few volunteers, the bus could also be used to help them with other errands and maybe take them on various outings.

Once a friendship has been established with a person living with disability, here is something you might try that meets both the needs for mobility and self-esteem and builds relationships. Men should do this with men and women with women. The friend living without disability calls and says, "I tell you what we're going to do today. You and I are going to the mall - but it is your day! We'll go into whatever store you want to visit. We'll look at anything you want to see. I will drive, and you buy us lunch." You might think, "Isn't it petty to ask a person with disability to pay for lunch?", not at all. By saying, "I'll drive, you buy lunch," you are changing the tenor of your relationship. You are not a caregiver, and they are not a person with a disability; you are two *friends* going to the mall.

Insecurity

Insecurity is a lack of self-confidence based on a lack of knowledge of one's identity, talents, and potential coupled with the inability to respond to, control, or cope with situations. In other words, a sudden infirmity will transformed an unsuspecting individual into a total stranger that he does not know. He becomes totally dependent on others to care for him, protect him, and help him build some kind of future.

Disability transforms an individual physically, psychologically, spiritually and emotionally. People with disabilities often face rebuilding their life from scratch. All at once they can lose their family, their vocation, their hobbies, and their future plans, and they have no idea whether or not they have what it takes to rebuild their life. They face a tomorrow full of very little except uncertainty. Uncertainty is present in every life, but most people live with a blissful illusion of control until a disaster turns their life upside down. When calamity comes, the victim awakens to the reality of uncertainty, and uncertainty creates an atmosphere of insecurity.

Not only does a person with a physical disability live at the mercy and convenience of others, he is also at the mercy of circumstances. There are many examples of how unpredictable circumstances can impact people with disabilities. Winter weather can be particularly dangerous and unforgiving. People have died of exposure because the lift mechanisms in their wheelchairs have frozen in mid-operation. One minister with a disability caught pneumonia after his wheelchair flipped over on an ice-covered ramp in route to church. He had to lie on the ice until help arrived.

What You Can Do to Battle Insecurity

In the midst of all of this unpredictability, people with physical disabilities need an anchor. They need "a soft place to fall." They need people and institutions in their life that will give them support, stability, and encouragement to believe that with the help of God and His people they can recover from any disaster and have a life that is full of joy. The answer is the local church. They need a pastor who will assure them that as long as God gives them breath, He has a plan and purpose for their lives. They need a church that will provide help and support when they are down, as well as encouragement and the opportunities they need to rise up and reach for their dreams.

Inferiority

After discovering how disability tends to dehumanize individuals and deprive them of a sense of their own personhood, it probably isn't surprising to learn that a person with a disability may be prone to tremendous feelings of inferiority. Physical disability is hard on self-esteem. Each physical disability presents unique challenges to maintaining a healthy self-image. Atrophy and disfigurement, drooling, the inability to speak normally, sexual dysfunction, progressive weakness, and countless other problems and conditions all eat away at one's self-esteem.

From the perspective of disability, feelings of inferiority are produced when someone judges their self-worth based on appearance, physical strength and ability, and weaknesses and limitations. In other words, personal value judgments are based solely on worldly standards. We live in a world that worships physical beauty, physical strength, and ability. When an individual is born without those characteristics, or becomes sick and loses health and strength, certain extreme segments of society begin to make harsh judgments and use phrases like "quality of life" and "ability to contribute." Babies diagnosed with severe disabilities in the womb are evaluated based on their assessed future quality of life. As a result, parents are sometimes given the option of having an abortion. A former governor of Colorado encouraged the infirm elderly and those with disabilities to "die and get out of the way" because they were using resources for which they could not pay.

These views are shared by abortion rights groups, euthanasia advocates, and bioethicists such as Dr. Peter Singer from Princeton who has written enthusiastically on the subject. One reviewer of his writings has said that it was fortunate that Dr. Singer was not in the delivery room the day Franklin Roosevelt and Helen Keller were born, or in the emergency room the night they brought in Christopher Reeve after he fell off his horse.

Thankfully, the Bible has a completely different perspective on human value. It is summarized in 1 Samuel 16:7, "*Do not consider his appearance or his height....The LORD does not look at the things man looks at. Man looks on the outward appearance, but the LORD looks on the heart.*" (NIV) God's perspective can be illustrated by "The Masterpiece Principle" which is based on how an appraiser evaluates an artistic masterpiece.

Typically, an appraiser will ask three questions. The first is, "Who created this work?" Each person on earth was touched by the creative hand of God while they were still in their mother's womb. In Psalm 139:13, 14, David declares, "*For you created my inmost being; You knit me together in my mother's womb. I praise you because I am fearfully and wonderfully made; Your works are wonderful, I know that full well.*" It is also important to recognize that David acknowledges imperfections due to the influence of sin from the time of conception (Psalm 51:5). Yet the touch of God overshadows those imperfections and provides correction just as a marred artistic work can be restored by a master artist.

The second question an appraiser asks is, "What materials were used in this work?" The Psalmist states that God created our inmost being. This refers to the "real" individual and not just our flesh and bones. It is the living spirit that contains our personality and leaves our body when we die. Genesis 2:7 says that God formed man, breathed into him the breath of life, and man became a living being. God originally intended for man to live forever. He gave man His own image and likeness (1:26, 27), and breathed into man His own Spirit. Man received the life of God so he could live forever, the light of God so he could be holy, and the love of God so that he could behave morally like God. All of that went out the window when man sinned. He died spiritually which is why Jesus said we must be born-again of the Spirit. When that happens, the light, life and love of God are restored to us because our once dead spirit lives again.

The third question the appraiser asks is, "How much will someone pay for this work?" God's answer is found in Romans 5 and in 1 Peter 1:18, 19. There we find that even though we were in a devastated and unrestored condition, God valued us so much that He sent His Son to redeem us through His death on the cross. We are worth far more than silver or gold to God.

Thus, we know that every individual has inestimable value because God was their Creator, He invested His own divine essence into the material used in the creation process, and Jesus Christ paid the ultimate price to reestablish man's relationship with God and give him eternal life. It is vital that this "masterpiece principle" be taught to every man, woman and child and not just to people with disabilities. It is the ultimate answer for a society plagued by self-esteem issues.

The Masterpiece Principle
Three reasons why every human being has value:
Even though flawed by sin, each person is the creation of
Almighty God
(Psalm 139:13-16).
They were made in God's image and likeness and infused with
His divine Spirit
(Genesis 1:26, 27; 2:7).

**While in a worthless spiritual state, they were redeemed by the precious blood of Christ
(1 Peter 1:18-19)**

What You Can Do Lessen Feelings of Inferiority

This Masterpiece Principle should be preached regularly from the pulpit and integrated into every level of the Christian education program in the church. More importantly, it should be put into practice in the ministry philosophy of the church. This can be accomplished by recognizing that people with disabilities are assets to the family of God and are not just people with problems and limitations who need to be cared for by others. People with disabilities are far greater than the sum of their problems and limitations. Like every person in the body of Christ, they have a gift that can be developed and a call they can fulfill if provided with encouragement, training and opportunity.

Insensitivity

Insensitivity is an interesting problem. The perceived inhumanity or ignorance of others has the cumulative effect of making a person with a disability feel "less than a person" or "just a piece of meat."

The fact is that a large segment of society misunderstands or is deliberately ignorant about the world of disability. It is also true that a much smaller segment of society is just plain mean or cruel. Some of these people may even work in the health-care or social-service professions. However, there is a common tendency for people with disabilities, especially in the early days or years of their disability experience, to have an exaggerated sense of their own tragedy which causes them to become *oversensitive* to the slights of others. Therefore, it is imperative for people with disabilities to learn to discern between perception and reality where the insensitivity of others is concerned.

The insensitivity of others towards a person with disabilities can be manifested in countless ways. The following **examples** can help us learn to distinguish the difference between cruelty and mean-spiritedness, insensitivity, and discomfort about interacting with people with disabilities.

You are a 15 year-old victim of a diving accident in the hospital undergoing rehab. It is midnight, and two brisk, efficient nurses, who are preoccupied with their own conversation, snap on the lights and begin to change your soiled sheets. You have been warned by the doctors and nurses in ICU and the rehab unit to make sure that you are turned gently and carefully because your spinal cord injury is still fresh. However, these two nurses seem to take a fiendish glee in turning their young male patients as quickly and roughly as possible as though they were playing some kind of game. When you protest, they laugh it off. From other patients you learn that some of them have been called names and others have been told to just shut up. This incident actually happened and is an example of genuine abuse and insensitivity at its most extreme. In every case, this kind of behavior should be dealt with as quickly and strenuously as possible. Although many complaints were lodged against these two nurses, one of them was actually permanently assigned to the spinal cord unit.

You have been to the clinic for a checkup. When your wife parked the car, she found a spot reserved for people with disabilities. In order to transfer you to the wheelchair on the passenger-side, she pulled in as close to the left side of the parking slot as possible. The gentleman in next parking slot on your right had to exit his vehicle on the driver's side with an oxygen apparatus, so he parked as far to the right as he possibly could. Two and one-half hours later, when you emerged from the clinic, it was 12:00 noon, and the parking lot was completely full. When you get to your car, you discover somebody with a compact had squeezed illegally into the space created between your car and the car in the next legal space. Your wife begins to sputter and turn red, not because of the noon heat, but because there is no longer room to transfer you from your wheelchair into the car! This is a real example of genuine insensitivity, and like the situation with the abusive nurses, it should be dealt with through the authorities.

You are in a restaurant with a number of friends, and you are all chatting when the waitress comes to take your order. It is obvious that your disability is mobility related, but instead of asking you for your order, the server asks one of your friends what you would like. If reports can be believed, incidents like this have probably offended millions. However, listening to some people with disabilities talk about their restaurant experiences might make you think that their poor server had kidnapped the Lindbergh baby. These types of incidents don't spring from ignorance, insensitivity, or a desire to hurt anyone. They are born out of a lack experience in communicating and interacting with people with disabilities. If a person with a disability responds with grace and good humor, the server can be educated, empowered, and won over to the cause of disability awareness rather than alienated and made to feel as if she had committed an unpardonable sin. The best solution to the "restaurant problem" is to find a little cafe and become a regular customer.

What Can You Do?

As noted earlier, people with disabilities need to establish a healthy perspective on their situation. As you build a friendship with a person who has a disability, you can help them to gain some perspective on the disaster that dismantled their life. The following three basic truths can help establish and build perspective:

- ☐ Everyone experiences tragedy.
- ☐ Situations are always relative. There will always be some who are better off than you and others who are worse off than you.
- ☐ God is always at work behind the scenes, and things will get better.

At the beginning of this section, we said that insensitivity is an interesting problem. One of the reasons it is so interesting is that for a person with a disability, the ultimate solution to the insensitivity of others is to develop a certain amount of insensitivity themselves. Tolerance, a sense of humor, maturity, God's grace, and the determination not to take oneself so seriously will allow a person with a disability to move graciously in the world.

Incapacity

Like inferiority, the prison bar of incapacity is created by a world that worships physical strength and ability, and divides people into two groups: the "can do" club and the "can't do" club. Incapacity becomes real when a person with a disability believes they are little more than a "broken toy" that has been "put up on a shelf." It is caused when value judgments are based on worldly standards, and it creates feelings of brokenness and uselessness that are manifested in three ways:

- ☐ The inability to approach the world from a position of strength and control.

- ☐ The inescapable feeling of being constantly overwhelmed.

- ☐ The inability to devise strategies to cope with one's life situation.

Over time, these negative attitudes can infect a person's life. However, there is an alternative view of incapacity. It was the perspective of a man who experienced more adversity in life than most. The dangers and challenges he faced in his life quest make the fictional adventures of escapist heroes limp, lame, lifeless, and laughable by comparison. This underrated man who understood physical hardships and failure so well was the apostle Paul (2 Cor. 11: 16-33). Paul was absolutely convinced by the witness of the Holy Spirit and his own life experience that the following three principles are eternally true:

- ☐ To be truly powerful and successful, a person must approach the world from a position of weakness so that all they have is the strength Christ provides (2 Cor. 12:9, 10).

- ☐ A Christian cannot know that they can do all things through Christ's strength unless they are willing to face those things that seem overwhelming. It is only when they commit to walking on stormy waves that they discover Christ will be their strength and support (Phil. 4:12, 13).

The problem facing those who minister to people with disabilities is not that the Church doesn't have the answers. The problem is developing an atmosphere where the person being ministered to is ready to receive those answers. We live in a world that cries and bleeds. It needs Jesus, but it will not be ready for Bible study until we dry their tears and take care of their wounds. James 2:14-17 says that when a person comes to your door cold and hungry, you can't solve their problem by simply saying, "be warm and be full," and send them away. You must get personally involved and meet their needs.

What You Can Do

There's a story about a man who falls into a hole and can't get out. A doctor walks by. The man in the hole cries out, "Hey Doc, I'm down in this hole, can you get me out?" The doctor stops, writes out a prescription, and tosses it into the hole. Soon a minister passes by. The man in the hole cries, "Hey Pastor, I'm down in this hole, can you get me out?" The minister stops beside the hole, says a prayer, and goes on his way. Finally the man in the hole sees a friend going by. He cries, "Hey Joe, I'm down in this hole, can you get me out?" Joe recognizes his friend and promptly jumps down into the hole. The poor guy in the hole goes ballistic. "What did you do that for? Now we're both stuck down here!" Joe replies, "Yeah, but I have been down here before, and I know the way out."

Unfortunately scriptures by themselves can become mere platitudes, but when coupled with the power of personal involvement and a victorious testimony of a caring friend, a person with a disability can be reconnected to the power and relevance of biblical truth.

Isolation

People with disabilities spend an inordinate amount of time alone. Isolation is a disconnection from routine and healthy human interaction and companionship. It is often caused by a combination of several factors working together. Medical complications of their disability may keep a person confined to their bed or to their home. They may not have the equipment they need such as a ramp, a lightweight or power-driven wheelchair, or transportation. Sometimes they may not have anyone to help them get out. Isolation may be psychological, emotional, spiritual, and/or physical. Often a person with a disability has the feeling of being "alone in a crowd."

Isolation may be actual or perceived. Sometimes people with disabilities have a chip on their shoulder or are so distracted by other "prison bars" that they fail to recognize when other people are reaching out to them. They may not intentionally ignore people who are trying to establish a friendship, but they miss the opportunity because they are so self-involved and preoccupied with trying to solve other problems.

The sense of isolation can be projected by misunderstanding, rejection, or the logistics of disability. Misunderstanding is much more common than actual rejection. The logistical problems a person with disability faces can be illustrated in the following example.

You are a college student who spends most of the day with the same group of classmates. They are your friends. They like and respect you, but when they grab a Coke and a burger downtown after class, they leave you behind because they only have 45 minutes. If you went along, it would take longer than that to get you in and out of the car and drive back and forth to the cafe.

What You Can Do

To end their isolation, a person with a disability needs a friend who is willing to invest the time and personal inconvenience it takes to get them out of the house and back into the game of life.

People with physical disabilities need understanding from those who work in disability recreational programs and ministries. Staff members at camp and retreat programs have sometimes wondered why people with physical disabilities seem to spend an inordinate amount of time talking together when they could be involved in recreational games or activities. People with physical disabilities often come to these programs after weeks or months of living in isolation and sometimes nearly complete solitude. While some may not participate in other activities out of trepidation or fear of failure, most are just craving conversation and good fellowship with people who live in situations similar to their own. The answer to drawing them into other activities is to start slowly and incorporate games and activities into their times of fellowship.

Insulation

Insulation is simply self-imposed isolation because of overwhelming feelings of insecurity, inferiority or fear of the unknown. Insulation's prison bar can only be broken by an individual's decision. If a friend invests time in creating an atmosphere of trust, they can be persuaded to venture out.

In Luke 14, the master of the feast sent his servants out to compel the disenfranchised to come to his house. Imagine for a moment that you are one of those who have been invited. You are probably a person who lives on the street, and you probably have not bathed for a while. Your clothes are dirty and tattered, and on top of that you may have a physical or mental disability. Faced with these circumstances, you would have to have trust that if you accepted the invitation to this grand party, you would not be embarrassed or made to look like a fool.

It is also important to recognize that the community of people with physical disabilities can be very cliquish. It is a very closed community. The only way to get in is to pay the price of admission and be impacted by a physical disability yourself or earn the right to be heard by being a patient and supportive friend.

What You Can Do

Insulation can be overcome through patience, understanding, encouragement, and a serious investment in the life of a person with a disability. An example of how this kind of investment can change a life and break the prison bars of Isolation and Insulation, check out the book and/or the movie, *A Man Called Norman* by evangelist and singer Mike Adkins.

Indignation

Indignation is perhaps the most insidious and self-destructive of the prison bars. It is a deep-seated, unresolved anger resulting from the inability to come to terms with things that one cannot change, and the inability to see the hand of God at work behind the scenes. In simplest terms, it is the inability or refusal to accept loss.

Naomi's story in the Book of Ruth is the best biblical example of this emotional state. Roughly translated, Naomi's name meant "life of the party." However, after catastrophe struck her life, Naomi blamed God and changed her name to "Mara" which meant "bitter." Bitterness is anger turned inward. When a person becomes so bitter that they change their name to "Bitter," they have become the embodiment of hardheartedness and indignation! Naomi failed to recognize that God was with her throughout her trial. It was Ruth's unconditional love that changed her perspective. The Church is the agent through which God's unconditional love is expressed to the world. It must become "Ruth" to the community of people with disabilities.

Grief and anger are legitimate facets of mourning loss. The problem is that disability is a multi-layered loss that sometimes manifests itself over several years. This is why it may take one to five years for a person to adjust to their new life.

What You Can Do

People who decide to invest their time in a friendship with a person living with a disability should prepare themselves for a rocky road. When the person with a disability realizes that you are for real and are a true and faithful friend, they may show you an ugly side of their disability that you did not expect. Expressing anger and learning how to resolve it is a legitimate stage in the grieving process. It is also a phase that many Christians try to avoid because they believe that expressing anger is a sign of weakness and sinfulness. However, repressed anger turns to bitterness, disillusionment, and ultimately unbelief in God's loving care.

A good tough friend can act as a sounding board to help the person with a disability confront and come to terms with their anger. Sooner or later, the anger must be dealt with before restoration can begin. People with disabilities need to know that God is big enough to handle their outrage and anger just as He did in the Bible with people like Naomi, David, Habakkuk, and Jonah. Not only can God handle their outrage, but He can help them resolve their anger, make peace with their situation, and place their future in His loving hands.

Inhibition of Relationships

Disability wreaks havoc on relationships. It alters, often irrevocably, every relationship an individual has. It is especially destructive when disability comes suddenly and savagely. Parents suddenly want to parent their adult children again. Fiancés are often counseled by medical personnel to walk away and not come back. Friends don't know where they fit in; they don't know whether they are helping too much or not enough.

Disability is hardest on marriages. For a time, and sometimes permanently, a spouse takes on the additional and difficult role of primary caregiver. Caregiving can be physically, emotionally, mentally and spiritually exhausting. Sometimes the wife of a husband who has a disability must go to work full-time for the first time. In addition to financially supporting the family and caring for her husband, she must still manage the home and do all her regular household tasks and chores.

Additionally, there are financial pressures and strains on the intimacy the couple once enjoyed. Many couples and families break under the unbearable strain disability brings into their life. It is very important that families have some kind of support from the local church, and organizations like Special Touch Ministry, Inc. There they can find someone who will listen and can meet others living in similar circumstances. Caregivers also need respite; they need times when they can completely get away from both the disability and its responsibilities. With compassion, support and understanding, families can find hope for their situation.

What You Can Do

Here are several things the local church can do to help people with disabilities strengthen their relationships with their families and other people:

- As you initiate a relationship with a person with a disability, be understanding and patient. Do not quit if your first efforts at friendship are rejected. Usually it is not personal. Often a person with a disability is just self-involved and preoccupied with trying to solve other problems, so "...try, try again."

- Do not make snap judgments about where a person or a family is at in the process of adjusting to or coping with life with a disability. The ones who seem well adjusted may be putting up a front, and those who seem to be struggling may be working through their issues in a healthy way by confronting them openly.

- [ ] Treat families impacted by disability as families; recognize that each member of the family has been affected by this situation to some degree.

- [ ] Encourage families to participate in activities designed for families with disabilities such as Special Touch Summer Get Aways and retreats.

- [ ] Provide financial assistance to families who wish to attend such functions but can't due to the lack of finances.

- [ ] If traditional pastoral counseling proves ineffective, a pastor should recommend professional Christian counseling.

- [ ] The church board could consider financially sponsoring such counseling if the family cannot afford to pay. Some Christian counselors work on a sliding scale or even do pro bono work for some needy families.

This list demonstrates that the answers are not always found in the local church. Therefore, the church needs to develop its role as a facilitator and make it their goal to help families affected by disability find the help that they need.

Inherent Sense of Failure and Shame

One measurement of success in life is the degree to which a person can contribute and make a difference. People with disabilities can carry a sense of failure and shame in their hearts. This comes from a lifestyle of being waited on and taken care of by others. They may also feel that they are a burden to others. In some cases, there is an inescapable and unbearable sense of self-condemnation because they live in an environment where they are always receiving and never giving.

For their own mental, emotional, spiritual, and in some cases, physical health, people with disabilities *must* be given opportunities to give of themselves. This means allowing and encouraging them to take risks and be willing to fail. Instead of hurting them, risking real failure actually sweetens the taste of success and helps restore a sense of wholeness.

Is there any better place to learn how to give to others than the local church? Absolutely not! The church is the perfect place for a person with a physical disability to find, develop and practice their gift and their call. Believe it or not, with the right adaptations, a person with a physical disability can serve in any ministry capacity in the church. All they need is the encouragement, the training, and the opportunity.

What You Can Do

Here are several ways in which the local church can help break this prison bar:

- ☐ Every church congregation should take a ministry gift inventory; most pastors have access to material that can be used to help people find their area of giftedness and ministry.

- ☐ Make sure that inaccessibility is not a barrier to a person developing their gift and fulfilling their call.

- ☐ If a person wants to try an unconventional method doing something, let them try. You would be surprised at how many people can play the guitar with their feet.

- ☐ Some people don't find their gift and their call immediately. You must keep encouraging them until they find their place and their purpose.

Inability to See Anything but the Bars

Dale Evans Rogers and her famous husband, Roy, adopted a boy with disabilities. In one of her books, Dale observed that living with a disability was like fighting Goliath with a broken sword on a daily basis. The most underappreciated fact about the world of disability is that it is "24/7/365" battle. There are no vacations. There are no breaks. Those who live with respirators or sleep in iron lungs struggle to draw their next breath. Those who have chronic phantom pain, such as paraplegics and quadriplegics, describe life like living waist-deep in a deep fryer. Over time, the bully of disability becomes relentless, and the daily struggle can cause a person with a disability to "wind down" and give up.

What You Can Do

When people with disabilities see only the pain and futility of their situation, they withdraw further from healthy social interaction and behaviors. They neglect their personal appearance and/or housekeeping chores. They take the kindness of others for granted and stop taking care of their daily business such as keeping up with their bills. When these signs are present, they need a friend to do a very difficult thing – provide a reality check. They need someone who will be bold enough and kind enough to confront them with the truth. The friend needs to compassionately but specifically tell them what he or she has observed. The friend also needs to point out that while disability is a difficult struggle, every person on earth faces times of pain and suffering in life.

Doing such intervention can be delicate and embarrassing for both parties, but the sooner it is done, the sooner the person with a disability will be restored. The most difficult thing for both parties is that because disability is 24/7/365, another intervention may be necessary down the road.

Strategies for Change

People who desire to minister to those with disabilities can begin by using a three-step approach:

- ☐ Engage: seek out people with disabilities in your community. Build a friendship with them.

- ☐ Edify: draw them into your local church family of believers.

- ☐ Empower: help them develop their gifts and their calling. Encourage them to find their place in the body of Christ.

Conclusion

Society tries to provide answers to the problems faced by people with disabilities, but their efforts often fall short. All the technological advances, all the social and vocational programs, and all the testimonies of the triumphant, do not compensate for the fact that a human being has been physically, spiritually, mentally, and emotionally violated. That violation must be dealt with before any other factors will make a difference. It is the spiritual aspect that society most often neglects. Only the Church of Jesus Christ has the answer that can fill the hole in a person's heart.

Joni Earickson Tada stated in her first book that she finally became a Christian because the people who were witnessing to her "earned the right to be heard" by first listening to her and becoming her friends.

Believers must be willing to enter into the heartache and humiliation of people with disabilities by becoming the eyes of Christ, the smile of Christ, the voice of Christ, the hands of Christ and the heart of Christ without prejudgment and condemnation. It requires unconditional love. People with disabilities may never have an answer to the question "Why me?" But when they experience the unconditional love of a friend, they can begin to believe in God's unfailing love. When they are reconnected to the love of God, people with disabilities have the key that will ultimately free them from the prison bars of disability.

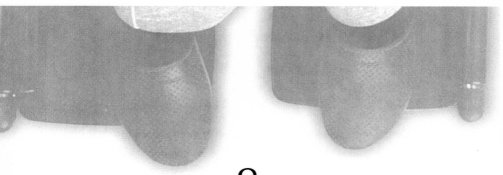

8.

The Crisis and the Covenant: The Impact of Physical Disability on Marriage

OBJECTIVES

- ☐ To develop an understanding of the impact of physical disability on marriage.

- ☐ To pinpoint factors that make the difference between success and splitting up.

- ☐ To discover practical strategies that can relieve the everyday pressures on a marriage impacted by disability.

- ☐ To learn about the joyful side of Christian marriage impacted by physical disability.

- ☐ To learn how the local church can minister to families impacted by physical disability.

THE CONCEPT

Over the course of a lifelong marriage, tragedy is almost inevitable. God designed marriage so two people would literally become "one flesh." What God brings together, God can keep together. What God did not bring together originally can be kept together if a couple will bring Jesus Christ into their marriage as the "third strand" that will keep them bound together even when their entire world is unraveling.

Foundation Scriptures

Matt. 19:5-6; Eph. 5:31-33; Eccl. 4:11-12

THE IMPACT OF PHYSICAL DISABILITY ON MARRIAGE

Just like individuals, no two couples come into the world of physical disability the same way, experience it the same way, or respond to it in the same way. However, there are some common emotions and circumstances that many couples will experience. This chapter focuses on the challenges most couples will face when confronted with physical disability.

Couples generally fall into two categories. The first group consists of those who married when disability was not a part of their life. Disability dropped on them suddenly and unexpectedly through an accident or illness. The second group is made up of those who married when a long-term physical disability was pre-existing. Although these couples have certain advantages, they also face unique challenges. This chapter applies to couples in both categories.

Physical disability, like other life shattering events, can wreak havoc and devastation on marriage relationships. Couples who are married prior to the occurrence of the disability are especially vulnerable, as are those in situations where the woman has a disability. The divorce rate for people with physical disabilities is significantly and consistently higher than the divorce rate of the general population according to the Multiple Sclerosis Web Site. Among the physical disabilities considered the most menacing to marriage are head trauma, multiple sclerosis, and spinal cord injury. Life with a long-term physical disability often brings even the most committed Christian couples to the brink of divorce, depression, and despair.

For those who manage to stay married, issues created by the presence of a disability can cause a physical and emotional gulf to exist between the two partners. While a couple wants to resolve the issues that isolate them from one another, they are reluctant to try. They are terrified of dredging up so much pain and poison that what little they have will be destroyed. In trying to protect what they have, they stay together, but they remain very much alone.

One woman whose husband suffers with multiple sclerosis aptly summarized the impact of disability on marriage this way, "My husband has clinical MS, but we both have MS." *Because the true nature of marriage makes a couple "one flesh," the impact of physical disability is never isolated or restricted to the partner who was actually diagnosed with the disability. The physical, mental, emotional and spiritual fallout of this life shattering situation affects both partners.*

Disability is a bully that loves to wrap itself around every aspect and moment of married life. This section will deal with eight different areas:

- ☐ Shattered expectations
- ☐ Role reversal and abdication
- ☐ The caregiving relationship
- ☐ Challenges to intimacy
- ☐ Logistics of having fun
- ☐ Financial stress
- ☐ Worldly philosophies and resolutions
- ☐ Marriage to people with pre-existing physical disabilities

The good news is that these couples can cling to the fact that disability doesn't have to have the last word on the quality or future of their relationship. Although physical disability can be one of the most difficult and destructive storms in life, there is absolutely nothing that takes God by surprise. In the end, the covenant was made to handle crises.

"My husband has clinical MS, but we both have MS."

Shattered Expectations

Almost everyone who dreams of being married one day looks forward to marriage with some kind of expectation. Having expectations is normal and natural. Even the most clear-eyed, conservative, and realistic of couples cannot help having certain expectations about what their new life together will be like. From childhood, individuals dream about meeting that special someone. Most young children have absorbed and accepted the living "happily ever after" concept. Even when couples go through premarital counseling, learn about the realities of the divorce rate, and are cautioned about what the vow "for better or for worse" really means, some residue of the Cinderella syndrome remains. While people expect that there will be speed bumps on the road to happiness, they never seem quite prepared to face the fact that a life-shattering disaster could happen to them.

The following are some of the common emotional reactions people have when faced with broken dreams and shattered expectations.

"It Wasn't Supposed to Be This Way!"

When life drops hydrogen bombs, they sometimes sound like a phone ringing in the middle of the night. When it explodes, it may sound a lot like a friend or stranger saying, "There has been an accident," or the voice of a family doctor or specialist saying, "It looks like multiple sclerosis." As the stunned listeners try to regroup, get used to a whole new life, and try to get beyond their own personal pain to reach out and support one another, they also have to cope with their own emotional rubble.

One of the first emotions that surfaces when expectations have been violated by disability is a deep pervasive anger—a feeling of being cheated and robbed of that to which they are rightfully entitled. Shattered expectations range from having 2.5 children to achieving a certain level of financial success and security. For engaged couples and newlyweds, perhaps the greatest shock is the loss of "breathing room" —time to grow into their marriage and enjoy each other without being confronted by a crisis that will touch and overshadow the rest of their lives. However, couples who have been married for several years before the onset of disability are far more likely to get a divorce because they cannot cope with the new situation and make the necessary adjustments to the radical changes in their physical and emotional relationship. Sometimes disability follows other disasters. One woman, whose husband was paralyzed after a mining accident, found herself fighting anger and bitterness because they had also just lost a baby. Her sense of grief and loss was multiplied and was often overwhelming.

Husbands who become disabled grieve over the profound change in their expectations and plans. One quadriplegic lamented to his wife, "It wasn't supposed to be this way! I wanted to take care of you!" The truth is that he still can, although years of adjustment may have to come first. In every marriage, couples have to adjust to being married to one another. In a marriage impacted by disability, both the husband and his wife also have to adjust to being married to the disability.

The married couple are not the only ones to struggle with feelings of anger and grief. These emotions often spread to the in-laws, and pop up in different ways. The parents of the spouse with the disability often feel protective of their child and become suspicious and afraid that the non-disabled spouse or fiancé will decide to leave. Conversely, the parent of the non-disabled spouse or fiancé may be angry at the person with a disability for being selfish and not releasing their son or daughter. If the couple is childless, the parents of the non-disabled spouse may be angry over being deprived of grandchildren.

In every marriage, couples have to adjust to being married to one another. In a marriage impacted by disability, both the husband and his wife also have to adjust to being married to the disability.

Shattered expectations encompass the area of parenting. People with disabilities who are unable to conceive or who will have difficulty carrying and delivering a child grieve over their inability to physically parent children. Men feel diminished as husbands and fathers because their disability clashes with their preconceptions of masculinity and manhood. If they do not have children, they have to seriously consider their options: adoption, artificial insemination, radical life-threatening medical treatment, or remaining childless. They probably never imagined they would have to face such choices, and working through them often generates more anger. One quadriplegic has said, "When your wife desires to bear a child more than anything in the world, it is a devastating thing to have to choose between depriving her of her dream and approving artificial insemination, which is to my way of thinking, the same as having another man's baby."

"When your wife desires to bear a child more than anything in the world, it is a devastating thing to have to choose between depriving her of her dream and approving artificial insemination, which is to my way of thinking, the same as having another man's baby."

Another husband, who was working through the long and expensive process of adoption said, "My wife was obsessed with completing the adoption application, and every time I looked at it, or we began to work on it, anger would begin to rise and grow inside me. I would become enraged at having to jump through so many hoops to get permission from some social worker or bureaucrat to be a dad. We had to fill out a fifty-page home study and take IQ and fitness tests when it seemed like every unwed girl around us was having an unwanted pregnancy. Not one of them had to take so much as a pop quiz before she got pregnant."

For these men, as well as those who are already fathers, other expectations are immediately threatened by the onset of disability. Unsure of their capability after rehabilitation, they don't know who they are or what they can offer as fathers. They are haunted by questions. "Will I be able to play catch or go fishing with my son? Will I be able to take my family camping?" Their real question is, "With this disability, will I be able to live up to my own standards and expectations of what it means to be a dad?"

Though many dads with disabilities struggle with mobility and medical issues that complicate fatherhood, there is one sub-group whose courage in the face of impossible circumstances is remarkable, monumental, and inspiring. This group is made up of men who are disabled by head trauma. Imagine having all of the instincts and inclinations of fatherhood and being fully and completely unable to act on them. You can hear what's going on, you can see what's going on, you can feel what's going on, you are in full possession of your intelligence, wit, and compassion, but you cannot speak, and you cannot reach out in the ways a father can who is unhindered by such a disability.

These men, and the families who stand by them, are examples for families everywhere. They are the ultimate examples of how a man with a disability can succeed as a husband and a father. Over time, the couple and their families develop subtle intimate ways of communicating and interacting. Together they are able to go beyond the tunnel vision of false expectations to create an atmosphere of love and support that can last a lifetime.

Women with disabilities, and women impacted by the disability of their husbands, go through a similar crisis. Much of a woman's identity and self-image often revolves around fulfilling her role in conceiving, bearing and raising children. The magnitude of such an awesome emotional and spiritual loss is almost impossible to effectively communicate. The maternal aspect of womanhood has frequently been mocked by modern radical feminists, but history tells us that motherhood has been an essential part of the value society traditionally placed on women. In ancient societies and biblical times, childless women were considered worthless and objects of scorn and ridicule. In the story of Rachel and Leah, having children was considered to be of greater value than being physically attractive. Rachel was the more beautiful of the two, but she cried out to God, "Give me children or I'll die!"

The maternal nature also plays in the identity and self-concept of most women. Logistical difficulties in parenting sometimes must be handled by other people. This can eat away at a woman's self-image and concept of motherhood. They question how they can spend time bonding with a child if they don't have the strength to hold them, the sensation needed to touch them, or the dexterity to take care of their simplest needs. Because these are the primary ways a mother nurtures her children and establishes a life connection with them, motherhood can become a nightmare for women with a disability. At first, women in this situation don't realize there are things that can be done to compensate for these limitations. Equipment and strategies exist that can help a mother with a disability successfully fulfill her role. The initial impact of a disability on the maternal nature is the feeling that they are more helpless than their baby, and this wonderful, blessed event was not supposed to turn out this way! Because of what physical disability can do to a woman sexually, reproductively, and maternally, it can deliver a crushing blow to her self-image, femininity, and seriously threaten her marriage.

Shattered expectations related to parenting can be so devastating and destructive, that engaged couples impacted by physical disability might want to seriously re-evaluate their reasons for getting married.

"I Didn't Sign up for This!"

Another common emotional response to shattered expectations is, "I didn't sign up for this!" This is most commonly felt by the spouse of the person with the disability. Specific numbers change constantly, but it is statistically true that the husbands of wives with disabilities leave their marriages more often than do wives whose husbands have disabilities. But it happens both ways.

One woman angrily said that she did not get married in order to become a nurse. From her point of view, she was suddenly plunged into an exhausting and overwhelming world she did not expect and was not prepared to enter as a newlywed—if she was ready for the possibility at all. Newlywed life is complicated enough without a disability. Usually a wife concentrates on organizing and managing her new home, adjusting to day-to-day life with a husband, and working at her job, if she has one. If her new husband has a serious physical disability, her life is instantly transformed into something much more complicated. On top of everything else, she must now be the primary income provider, financial manager, social planner and at least a part-time caregiver.

Confronted by the constant demands that forcefully hold their heads under water, women often see escape from the marriage as the only way they can survive physically, mentally and emotionally. In much the same way, men feel totally incapable of caring for a wife with a disability. Even though they may still love their mate with all their heart, they do not see how they can fit into the new equation that has become their life.

When head trauma or Alzheimer's disease changes the personality of a spouse, some partners leave the marriage saying that their vows no longer apply because, "This is not the person I married!"

"It Isn't Like It Was!"

This emotional declaration is often made by those who were married prior to the onset of disability. Disability backlashes couples who to this point in their relationship have had most of their storybook expectations come true. It is the heart's cry of all of those who wish they could turn back the clock before disability broke down the door of their life and moved in. Spouses in this situation frequently divorce because they cannot adjust to either their new role or to the sexual dysfunction of their marriage partner. Couples who were engaged when the disability struck are more likely to have successful and lasting marriages than those who were already married.

The False Support of Others

Doctors, nurses and social workers are so aware of the destructive power of disability on marital expectations that they often make it a policy to counsel non-disabled spouses or significant others to immediately walk away from their loved ones. Because of the statistical realities, these rehabilitation professionals believe it is more merciful to walk away at the outset of life with a disability rather than later.

Expectation issues are further complicated by ignorant comments made by friends, relatives and others outside the relationship. Observers often characterize the willingness of a spouse to stay with his or her partner with a disability as "noble," "martyrdom," "unrealistic idealism," or just "stubborn stupidity." Likewise, they characterize the spouse with the disability as "selfish," "single-minded" and "unwilling to let go and face reality." Aside from being demeaning, negative, and non-productive, comments like this are based on false assumptions.

One woman becomes infuriated when someone calls her "special" or "noble" for marrying and staying with her husband. "It makes me so mad because people think they're being kind when they're really being patronizing and ignorant. They don't know what they're talking about, and they make several false assumptions. The first is that I married my husband out of pity. *The truth is I married my husband because I love him, and I didn't want to marry anyone else. It was my choice; no one twisted my arm. They also assume my husband has nothing to offer or give, and that I do all the giving, and he does all the taking in the relationship. That's just not true. Finally, they assume that a marriage impacted by physical disability cannot possibly be physically, emotionally, and spiritually fulfilling, and that's just not true either."*

"I am not noble or self-sacrificing. I did not marry my husband out of pity. The truth is I married my husband because I love him and I didn't want to marry anyone else."

Role Reversal and Abdication

Physical disability can force couples to surrender the roles they planned on fulfilling in their relationship. It forces them into new positions they often find unexpected, uncomfortable and undesirable especially in relationships where roles are rigidly and traditionally defined and where there are definite expectations about who will be doing what. A very young couple may still have an immature or undeveloped view of roles within a marriage. A husband with a disability may have expected that he would be out every day working at his job and pursuing his career while his wife may have expected to be at home managing the household and raising children. When disability strikes older marriages, a kind of cultural whiplash can take place. Suddenly after years spent in their own comfort zones, both marriage partners are forced to take on new and radically different roles and responsibilities.

Role reversal happens most frequently in marriages where a husband becomes disabled and his wife has to take on new, expanded roles and responsibilities. Often the man will eventually find himself taking on responsibilities he thought would belong to his wife such as vacuuming, dusting, washing dishes, doing laundry and getting supper ready. These are not bad things in and of themselves; they are important chores that need to be done. It is a good thing for a husband with a disability to learn these skills as a part of reclaiming and rebuilding his life. One quadriplegic found that relearning housekeeping skills was empowering and gave him a sense of control over his environment. Taking over the housekeeping role allowed him to have a sense of making a contribution. It also took some pressure off of his wife.

One husband with a disability referred to role reversal as: "The feeling of going through life with my pants on backwards."

Role reversal often creates mutual frustration. In the case where the husband has a serious physical disability, a wife can become frustrated and exhausted from having to take the major leadership role in the relationship. In addition to the nest builder, nurturer and homemaker, she may now also be the primary wage earner and caregiver, in addition to possible roles as financial manager, gardener, groundskeeper, carpenter, plumber, driver, packer, wheelchair mechanic, and Jill-of-all-trades. *She will be frustrated by her inability to balance all of these jobs, do them well, and still have time for church activities, ministry, hobbies, friends, and personal growth. It is a no-win proposition because she has far more tasks to accomplish and roles to fulfill than she has time, strength, or energy. She ends up feeling like she can't do anything right or please anyone.*

Meanwhile, her husband struggles to identify just what his role is in their relationship. Because he is unable to fulfill his traditionally expected roles as a husband and provider, he may feel diminished, emasculated and adrift. Since his wife now carries most of the responsibilities, the husband can often feel that he no longer has a vote or a right to express an opinion regarding how things should be done. The situation is aggravated because the wife is forced to get help from their friends and relatives in order to get things done. The natural result is that when the wife has a question, she may go to one of their friends or relatives for advice rather than asking her husband. This creates feelings of displacement and irrelevance, feeds his anger, and helps build a wall of resentment

One husband in this position said, *"We had a huge fight over this. I felt like everybody's opinion was more valuable than mine just because they could physically fix the screen door, start a snow blower, and change the oil on the car. I couldn't work or support my family; I couldn't give her children. I couldn't take care of my home, and now my wife wouldn't even come to me first for an opinion. I felt displaced, irrelevant, worthless and completely unnecessary."*

Disability and the role reversal issues it creates differ from many marital problems because they cannot simply be solved by communication alone. One victim of spinal-cord injury was discouraged because he was stuck day after day washing dishes and vacuuming while his wife was out earning a paycheck. He was further frustrated because, after spending the day all by himself, he was looking forward to a romantic evening. However, after working all day, cooking dinner, getting everything ready for the next day, and managing her husband's evening care issues, the wife wants nothing more than a soft pillow and a long night's sleep. Communicating about this problem will probably only make things worse before it will make it better.

Abdication occurs when one or both partners feel so overwhelmed that they give up on fulfilling their legitimate roles and responsibilities in the relationship. This often occurs when a man or woman is left at home with a profound disability, nothing to do during the day, and no immediate goals or the means to carry them out. Picture disability as a big, overwhelming bully sitting on a person's chest, shaking its finger in his face, and screaming, "You can't!" Eventually the person with a disability takes this message to heart and internalizes it as "I can't!" Then they are tempted to surrender to the bully and abdicate their role and responsibility in the relationship.

The bottom line is the wife feels overextended, underappreciated, overstressed, overburdened, discouraged and depressed while the husband feels diminished, distant, lost, angry, useless, unfulfilled and uncommunicative. They are so overcome by their misery and focused on the overwhelming aspects of disability that they fail to see the way out of their wilderness. The answers to these problems lay in sitting down together, clearing the air of predetermined expectations, and either establishing new roles and responsibilities or devising strategies so that they can fulfill their existing roles without driving themselves insane or making each other crazy in the process.

In addition, they need to make a five-year plan for rehabilitation and education which will ultimately allow the husband to fulfill his desire to provide for his family and meet vocational goals. He should have tasks he can complete daily which will give him a sense of productivity and mastery over different aspects of his disability. Instead of bemoaning the fact that he cannot hold a job at the moment, he has to recognize his job is to gain the knowledge and master the activities of daily living and work skills necessary for him to become employable again.

Role issues also occur in marriages where the wife has a disability. If a housekeeper or nanny has to take over the jobs of homemaking and child-rearing, the wife can feel useless and empty. As they make decisions that go along with their responsibilities, the wife can feel as though her authority to manage her own home has been stripped away and lost. When these issues are combined with challenges to intimacy, she may begin to feel like a total non-entity. It is up to her husband to come to her rescue and to support and under gird her. He needs to constantly reaffirm her value as a person and a partner and reinforce her position and authority in their home with regard to people who are helping whether they are employees or relatives.

The Caregiving Relationship

Another major stress factor in marriages impacted by physical disability is the caregiving relationship.

The Burden of Caregiving

This is an interesting topic because the burden involved in caregiving varies according to the individual. Some absolutely refuse to have anything to do with caregiving. Others, especially women, have no problem being a caregiver; they look at caregiving as a natural part of being a woman and a wife.

The wife of a C-5 quadriplegic described her attitude toward caregiving by sharing what happened in a hospital when her husband was critically ill. The hospital staff did not want her to stay in the room and see to his basic comfort. Until she insisted, they wanted her to wait outside. With tear-filled eyes and fire in her voice, she stated, "That precious man was lying there battling for his life. There was so much I *couldn't* do to help him, to let him know I was with him, but I did know how to manage his personal care and attend to his comfort. That was a job no one could do better than me, so I insisted that they let me do it!" To her, caregiving was not a burden; it was her rightful role and his hospital bedside was the appropriate place for her to be.

Another woman who had been married to her husband for over forty years had to have her access and her right to give care written into her husband's orders when he was hospitalized for pneumonia. Her husband's physician realized she was an asset to the staff and essential to her husband's recovery. No one knew how to care for his needs as well as she could, and her husband was in a position where he could not direct his own care. This woman did not feel burdened or put upon. She felt strongly being his care provider was her right and privilege after forty years of marriage. When residents and nurses would get in her way her attitude was, "Just try and stop me!"

Stress for all of these women is not created by the caregiving. It is simply that they have too many areas of responsibility that they are supposed to take care of at the same time. Their husbands can unknowingly add to their stress by not receiving the ministry of their wives with grace and gratitude. That creates a collision between a husband's masculine self-reliance and the unconditional love of his wife. The husband with a disability can feel guilty because his wife "has to do" his personal care. While the wife considers it an informed choice which she opted to make voluntarily, the husband may see himself as a burden. He is actually creating a problem where one does not exist.

One study on the MS web site reports that one year after a spinal cord injury, most patients feel better about themselves and their situation emotionally, but their caregiver is more likely to feel worse emotionally than they did at the onset of the disability. Even for committed caregivers, exhaustion and depression can become serious issues if they don't get some kind of regular relief.

There are also men and women who just don't believe they are cut out to be personal care providers. They can't get beyond the idea of dealing with excrement, bodily fluids, and washing private parts of the human body. The truth is personal care is something most people can learn to do if they will consider it a service unto the Lord. If they need training on how to perform certain procedures, they can get help from their health-care provider or from many disability ministries.

The Indignity of Caregiving

Sometimes the spouse with a disability is uncomfortable with their partner providing care because of the indignity of the process. They feel guilty because their spouse has to labor day-after-day in the trenches of caregiving, confronting the ugly side of disability with all of its messes and smells. They are embarrassed when they have to remove the veil of privacy and dignity; it is hard to reveal their weakness and infirmity to another person.

Part of this issue is related to the way courtship works. People who are courting present themselves to one another in the best possible light. They put their best foot forward and try to look and smell their very best for one another. People with disabilities often have self-image issues involving their physical bodies. They may have muscular atrophy, weight problems, and/or disfigurements that can be camouflaged and disguised by clothing, but during caregiving and marriage, these physical problems become apparent. To put it another way, the indignity of disability can become the enemy of romance.

The answer to this problem is communication. A person with a disability may have all kinds of false preconceptions about how their spouse is going to feel about a body that has been rearranged by their condition. Their partner might not feel that way at all. They need to talk it through.

The Control of Caregiving

The battle over caregiving control is another area in which people with a disability can complicate the issue of caregiving and make it more difficult. During the rehabilitation process, they are indoctrinated with the idea that they are responsible to manage and direct their own care. This is a good thing. It teaches them that disability does not disqualify them from taking personal responsibility for maintaining their health and hygiene. At this early point in the disability experience, patients are often tempted to check out and abdicate all personal responsibility. So the indoctrination they receive during rehab is vital to their recovery and the process of reclaiming ownership of their life.

The problem comes when they get married and their spouse becomes their caregiver. When they begin to question and direct their spouse like they would any other health aide or attendant, the caregiving partners often take offense. They feel they are compassionate and competent. They don't want to be questioned, managed or directed; they just want their spouse to relax and receive their ministry. The spouse with a disability feels like if they can't manage their care and have input into the process, they are being treated like a patient, a passenger and a vegetable.

Looking at the situation objectively, both sides make legitimate points. The best way for couples to settle the issue of control is to sit down together, share their viewpoints with one another, and come to some middle ground so both parties can feel validated.

Challenges to Intimacy

Disability challenges marital intimacy on several levels but the point has to be made that joyful and fulfilling marital intimacy is possible in a marriage touched by physical disability. One man with a spinal cord injury commented, "Many times being together is so spontaneously joyful that I completely forget I have a disability."

Disabling physical impairment, medications, and other factors can complicate physical intimacy. These difficulties can be overcome by a willingness to approach the problem with honesty, maturity, patience, and humor. There is a lot of information available on how to work through these problems. The first resource a couple might access is their family doctor.

The truth is that the mechanics of sexuality are usually not the most difficult part of this issue. Physical complications have emotional consequences. One wife of a quadriplegic with multiple problems described it very poignantly. *"The hardest part of dealing with disability is not the caregiving and cleaning up bodily waste and other messes. It isn't the exhausting days and sleepless nights from having to get up several times during the night to turn him, or attend to plumbing that comes apart and gets the bed wet. The hardest part is knowing that when I get into bed with my husband, even if I am stark naked, he is barely aware of my presence because he can hardly see me, hear me, or feel my hand when I touch most of his body. He can't feel me next to him. The hardest thing about disability is getting into bed next to my husband and feeling like I am not even there. Knowing he can't even hear me cry makes it hurt even more."*

Physical complications have emotional consequences.

Physical complications have emotional consequences in the form of feelings. If those feelings are not communicated so that the couple

132

can work on the problem, the wife will begin to withdraw emotionally because the emotional part of intimacy is so painful. When she withdraws emotionally, she will also pull back physically which will create a frostiness in their relationship that will carry over to the next morning and every morning after that until the issue is resolved.

The husband can also create emotional distance through the anger he can bring into the bedroom from unresolved hostility toward his physical condition. In a sense, he hates his own body, and this cannot help but have a destructive effect on his relationship with his wife. The situation only becomes worse if he allows his disability to dictate his feelings about his manhood and masculinity. One paralyzed husband said, "Our love life became driven by my wife's need to get pregnant or by her hormonal clock. I felt like there was no emotional connection, romantic relationship, or celebration of a covenant. I felt hollow and empty. I felt like I was being used."

The answer to these angry feelings is to quit being self-absorbed and focus on adoring and cherishing his wife and fulfilling her needs. This starts with communication. If he is able to open up transparent communication so she can share her true feelings, they are on the way to fixing things up. This process must begin with the husband. He has to put his wife's need for mature dialogue and open communication ahead of his own needs. Wives won't start the dialogue because they don't want to hurt their husband's feelings.

If the husband with a disability wants to have free-flowing physical and emotional intimacy in his marriage he is going to have to grow up, leave the planet Mars, move back to Earth, and face these issues with the unconditional compassion and love of Christ that a spiritually mature Christian husband is called to lavish on his wife.

In the case of a man who is married to a woman with a physical disability, it again falls on the husband to take the lead and minister to his wife, cherishing her as his does his own flesh. While lavishing unconditional love upon her, he will rebuild the spiritual and emotional foundations of her femininity and sexuality that physical intimacy rests upon. After those foundations have been rebuilt, the couple can explore together the many resources that deal with the details of physical intimacy for couples impacted by disability.

Long Term Complications to Intimacy

There are two factors that can bring sexual intimacy to a long-term standstill or a permanent stop. The first are physical changes in the disabled spouse or in the non-disabled spouse, or both as they journey through life together. The second thief, that has already been alluded to is depression. Whichever spouse is dealing with it at the time, both will be impacted. Depression is an intimacy killer and it does so on almost all levels. There is no magic cure-all and no easy road back. *One thing is certain. Life is seasonal. If a couple impacted by physical disability is having a season of tremendous intimacy they should be careful to cherish it and not take it for granted. They must not be led into thinking that they can put off their opportunities and bank them for the future because the future is far from certain.*

Logistics of Having Fun

Studies and statistics show that having fun is a key element that keeps couples touched by physical disability together. However, when people are dealing with physical disability having fun is not always as easy as it seems. Ken and Joni Earickson-Tada's experiences illustrate how difficult having fun can be. One of their early dates was at Disneyland. They had a wonderful, fun-filled day together and enjoyed many of the rides. When Joni got home, she found that the physical pounding she had taken on the rides had opened up one of her pressure sores, and she was forced to remain in bed for many weeks. The same thing happened on their honeymoon when she sat too long on the plane.

After they were married, Ken wanted to plan a special, intimate evening for the two of them at home with music and candlelight in front of the fireplace. He prepared everything. He arranged for dinner. He fixed the lights. He turned on the music. He arranged himself and his wife comfortably in front of the fireplace, but it in the end it all fell apart. He began to talk about how every time they tried to have fun or do something special; it was complicated by the logistics of the disability. The disability always acted as a spoiler to their having a good time and enjoying each other. Unfortunately, when spouses begin talking frankly about what a pain disability can be, the spouse with the disability can begin to take it personally because they have become the personification of the disability. So Joni replied to Ken, "That's okay, sometimes I don't like you either". The danger is that this kind of talk can degenerate into a miserable descending spiral that ends with the question, "Why did we get married in the first place?"

Spontaneous problems related to disability can also spoil social and recreational plans. One couple had to change plans abruptly when the man was suddenly struck with diarrhea ten minutes before getting into a swimming pool. Several years later, the same couple had tickets to see the legendary Christian artist Dallas Holm who was appearing down the street from their home. Five minutes before going out the door, of the husband got sick and was forced to stay home. He urged his family to go to the concert anyway. However, sometimes when a non-disabled spouse chooses to go to an event or accept a social invitation alone, it triggers an argument, especially in new marriages.

Logistical problems aren't always a bad thing. This writer, a quadriplegic since 1983 and a person with mild cerebral palsy since birth, says sometimes logistical difficulties and the unexpected make an occasion more fun and more memorable.

Early in our marriage, we went on a one-day canoe trip with the young-married couples group in our church. I was nervous about the whole thing from the very beginning. When we got there, they discovered it was going to be very difficult to get me and my wheelchair down to the canoe because we had to park the cars in a lot at the top of a hill. Fortunately, one of the guys was a captain in the Army so he took charge. He decided the easiest thing would be to put me in the canoe while it was at the top of the hill, and then simply push the canoe down the hill with me in it. They put me on a chaise lounge-style lawn chair so I could sit up easily. When they launched the canoe, the chaise lounge went flat, and all I saw was blue sky as the canoe went bumpity, bumpity, bumpity down the hill. I don't exactly know what happened next, but I heard someone shout, "He's floating down the river!" Then I heard my wife yell, "I'll get him!" Next I heard a big splash. In her hurry to catch me, Gayle had slipped and fallen into the water. That was just the beginning to one of the most fun-filled days we have ever had. Laughing with people, laughing at ourselves, and stretching our boundaries was very empowering. Another time a couple of friends stuffed me into a four-seater airplane..."

Fun in the face of disability is often mixed with a bit of terror because of the unpredictability of it all. One person said, "Every day is a day at Disney World when you have a disability because you have no idea what kind of wild ride the day will bring." In the end, however, the terror usually has been conquered, and a good time has been had by all. This fact lead one wife to quote a Gracie Allen line from an old movie, "It's fun having fun even if you don't enjoy it".

Financial Stress

Disability is not cheap. Medications, equipment, supplies, transportation, and adaptations for the home can add hundreds or even thousands of dollars to a family's monthly budget. On top of that, many families dealing with disability have financial trouble because they have lost the income of the spouse with the disability. A 1998, a Louis Harris poll in conjunction with the National Organization on Disability showed that one-third of all households dealing with physical disability have an annual income level of less than $15,000. Fortunately as of this writing, most counties and states have programs that can help families dealing with disabilities get most of the things they need including medical assistance and vocational rehabilitation programs.

Many families live month-to-month and cannot afford to frequently update or replace their equipment. While county and state programs can help with much of this, the family may have to be on a waiting list before they can begin to receive county services. Typically the waiting period can be five years or longer. As budget cuts are made, and more and more people sign up for less and less money, fewer of their expenses are covered, and their stack of non-covered medical bills gets higher and higher.

Couples usually try to make do by purchasing used wheelchairs, medical equipment, and used vehicles. However economizing like this creates its own problems. Insurance companies won't cover repairs or maintenance on used or privately-purchased equipment. Even minor repairs and maintenance can run into hundreds or thousands of dollars.

Even programs designed to help people with disabilities can entangle them in a bureaucratic Catch-22 situation. People with disabilities often have access to multiple programs that will cover disability conversion on a vehicle. This is a good thing because disability conversion can cost as much as the vehicle itself. The problem is that, except for an occasional private endowment, grass-roots community project, or benevolent service group, very few sources will subsidize the vehicle itself. These sources are rare because the cost of vehicles is astronomical in relation to the amount of money they can raise and the number of people who come to them for help. People with disabilities can usually afford an older vehicle, but conversion companies usually won't convert them due to structural problems, and the insurance companies won't pay for it anyway.

Having to deal with this kind of frustration and constant penny pinching leaves few funds for frills and fun and over time has a tendency to let the air out of life. A local church can help relieve some of the financial stress by providing sponsorship funds for couples and families to attend Christian camps and retreat programs designed for people with physical disabilities.

Worldly Philosophies and Resolutions

Complicating and compounding the problems disability brings into a marriage are the worldly philosophies and resolutions offered by social workers, medical professionals, and at times even relatives and Christian friends. *Invariably their so-called counsel and advice minimizes a couple's Christian convictions, disregards God's place in the relationship, and dismisses the meaning of holy vows made before God.* Some of the counsel couples receive is as follows:

"Live together for two years before you get married."

Rehabilitation professionals have a guarded or "cautiously negative" view of marriage when it comes to their patients and clients with disabilities. In all fairness, they live in the world of statistical probabilities and from a purely worldly and statistical point of view, the probabilities of a long-term, successful marriage for people dealing with disability are terrible. From their perspective, these professionals are trying to protect the emotional and psychological well-being of their clients and patients. They believe they are exercising good judgment, offering wise counsel, and acting with compassion. Their rationale for giving this advice is, "Living together gives both of you an escape hatch if things don't work out."

The problem is that Christian marriage, by its very nature, is an unconditional lifelong commitment to love and cherish another person with the help of God in the face of any circumstance. Life is unpredictable, and trouble is a foregone conclusion and absolute certainty. Just what conditions are acceptable for either partner to use an escape hatch? Biblically speaking, God designed Christian marriage as a blood covenant sworn before God. Such covenants were not to be entered into lightly, and they were not to be revoked.

Adopting a worldly "escape hatch" philosophy creates a self-fulfilling prophecy for marital failure.

This total lack of understanding of the biblical view of marriage is reflected in other advice given to those living with disability by the secular world of social work and rehab medicine.

> "At least work out the physical complications of disability in the marriage relationship in our special room down the hall for a weekend."

This was advice was actually given to a couple who was going to get married ten days after the groom's discharge from rehab. The prospective groom commented, "Sometimes it was as if there was a deliberate, concentrated effort on the part of some staff members, at all different levels, to get us to compromise our Christian convictions. It wasn't about trying to help us adjust to marital life with a disability; it was about getting us to compromise."

A doctor told the same couple, "You might as well get married; you can always get a divorce." These people may know a lot about rehabilitation and medicine, but they fail miserably in understanding that the "escape hatch" philosophy, more often than not, creates a self-fulfilling prophecy of marital failure. On the other hand, making an informed, empowered, holy, and lifelong commitment helps a couple keep their commitment.

Marriage to People with Long-term, Pre-existing Physical Disabilities

Someone who chooses to fall in love and marry a person with a pre-existing physical disability has some distinct advantages compared to the person who comes into the world of physical disability suddenly and unexpectedly; but they still face unique challenges of their own. The advantage lies in that the prospective spouse has time to learn on a certain level what it is like to accommodate disability in a relationship. During the dating process, they may also learn some attendant skills. All of this allows them to become comfortable with physical disability at their own pace.

Another advantage is that the person with a disability has probably become comfortable to some degree with their disability and may have gained a certain amount of control over its domination in their life. However that comfort and control was designed to meet the needs of a single person living alone. From the point of view of a marriage partner, that same comfort and control may appear demanding and inflexible. The spouse with the disability is not only used to being the center of their world, they are used to being its absolute monarch. They are accustomed to being an employer working with employees who must perform to an acceptable standard or be fired. The person with the disability can say what he wants done, where he wants it done, how he wants it done, and when he wants it done. Exercising that kind of dictatorship is perfectly acceptable in an employer-employee relationship. But no matter how politely it is phrased, demanding control doesn't work very long in a healthy marriage. *In a good marriage, the person with a disability must learn to balance the urgency of meeting their own needs against the needs of their marriage partner.*

A fiancée who may have been perfectly comfortable with the disability during the courtship may feel unprepared, overwhelmed, exhausted, and ready to scream once they are married for a while. The problem isn't that the spouse with the disability is an evil, unfeeling tyrant, it's just that he is not used to having things any other way. He needs to be put on notice that this is a marriage and not a business arrangement. Through discussion, negotiation, and compromise the couple can work out an understanding that makes the marriage work for both of them.

If the person with the disability cannot give up their throne and cherish and adore their husband or wife the way they should, the spouse is going to start to ask this question: "What you did you marry me for anyway? If you just needed a housekeeper, a cook, a nurse, a driver and a prostitute you should have hired them instead of marrying me!"

Biblical Principles That Make the Difference between Success and Splitting Up

Counting the Cost

Every couple planning to get married needs to look at marriage and the marriage vows with their eyes wide open. There is no guarantee that marriage will bring the fulfillment of any dream either one of them may have; there is only a lifetime of possibilities. On the other hand, there is a one hundred percent chance that they will have problems, challenges, and trouble to some degree. *In Matthew 6:34, Jesus said that each day brings trouble of its own, and in John 16:33, He confirmed that each of us would experience trouble in this world. Every family will experience trouble and disasters throughout the course of their life time, and couples need to know this is an absolute certainty from the start. They definitely will not be the only couple in all of human history that will have a trouble-free life and marriage.*

When couples have a mature understanding of what Christian marriage really is, they are able to make mature decisions even when catastrophe strikes before they walk down the aisle. One bride was asked why she wanted to go through with the wedding when her fiancé became a quadriplegic during their engagement. She replied, "What would I have done after taking my vow before God if he had become hurt the week after the wedding?" Because she had a complete and mature understanding of her wedding vows during her engagement, she was able to make an informed decision.

Another fact couples need to evaluate is that everyone brings baggage into marriage that must be addressed. It may be disability, fertility problems, clinical depression or a thousand other possibilities. Couples that take an honest look at each other and really count the cost will come to one of two conclusions. *They will either walk away before going down the aisle, or they will take one another in hand and say, "No matter what baggage you may bring or what situation may arise, I would rather walk through the challenges of life with you than to live without you."*

There is a positive side to knowing there will be problems and trouble in life. First of all, it brings to light one of the best reasons for getting married. Everyone, whether married or single, will experience difficulties in life. Having a friend, companion, lover, and partner who brings Christ's unconditional love and a lifetime commitment to the relationship can be a sustaining force and a gift from God as you face these challenges together. Secondly, when Jesus promised in John 16 that there would be trouble in this world, He also said: *"Be of good cheer. I have overcome the world."* He becomes the third strand in the cord which makes it much stronger than a cord with only two strands (Ecc. 4:12). Staying connected to Jesus is the secret to overcoming all the land mines in life including physical disability in marriage.

The bottom line of any Christian marriage should be: "No matter what baggage you may bring or situation that may arise, I would rather walk through the challenges of life with you than to live without you."

Faithfulness

Mature believers will understand a few things about biblical faithfulness that could save most marriages that have trouble. In the world, many people are ready to bail out on their marriage when times are rough or feelings began to fade or change. The Bible teaches in Ecclesiastes and other places that life is seasonal. Even in the best marriages, feelings will ebb and flow, rise and fall, and rise again. Feelings must not be confused with love itself. True love is a choice while feelings change with circumstances, environment, and other factors. That is the nature of all relationships. This can be illustrated by God's relationship with us. God's love for His people is unconditional, but as they live their lives before Him, the triune Godhead can be pleased, angry, grieved or delighted with our behavior and attitude. True love and commitment don't bail when feelings, circumstances, or seasons change because they are transitory and will change again. Real love and commitment are not stopped or cut off by the changing seasons in life; they carry a couple through those seasonal changes.

Mature believers keep Jesus Christ and His Word at the center of their relationship. They make Him the "the third strand" in the cord that binds them together as a couple and empowers them to be faithful to their wedding vows. They make the Word of God the source of their strength. The Word reminds them that they can do all things through Christ who strengthens them (Phil. 4:13). A couple must always remember that God will never put anything more in their life than they are able to bear (1 Cor. 10:13; 2 Cor. 12:9).

Forgiveness

The potential for petty disputes and misunderstandings is so great in a marriage, that it is imperative couples make the Cross of Jesus Christ the cornerstone of their relationship. This is true for every marriage, but it is even more critically so for couples impacted by physical disability. A couple needs to have a continuous source of forgiveness in their home so that they can resolve disputes both large and small. When forgiveness dries up, bad things start to happen. Molehills become mountains, and communication shuts down. Being able to flow in the forgiveness that comes from the Cross of Christ is what keeps the marital train on the tracks.

Gratitude

1 Thessalonians 5:18 reminds us that it is God's will that every Christian gives thanks in every circumstance. When you openly, constantly, and enthusiastically express thanksgiving for the presence of God, for every blessing that comes from God, for every kindness bestowed by friends and others, and for the love of God that sustains marriages and families, you are creating a positive atmosphere in your home and marriage.

Every Christian marriage can survive if the couple will make forgiveness and the cross of Jesus Christ the cornerstone of their relationship.

Kindness

One day, a paraplegic man heard a preacher on Christian television make a declaration that changed both his attitude and his life. The preacher roared, "'Be ye kind one to another is the law of God!'" By continually reminding himself of that simple law, this man changed the tone and atmosphere of his heart and home. Embracing that law changed the emotional temperature and the dynamics of almost every area we've discussed in this chapter. "Suddenly," he stated, "the problems of my disability were no longer constantly pressuring me because I was no longer the center of my world. The law of kindness requires that other people come first."

There is a tiny voice in the heart of many people with disabilities that tells them they are a victim and what happened to them was totally and completely unfair. As long as that voice speaks, it will ignite and give off tiny, almost microscopic sparks of anger and self-pity. In a home and family, these negative emotional sparks translate into irritability, unkindness, and self-centeredness which produce only grudging cooperation and overall resentment in family members.

Sometimes it can take years to come to grips with all of the physical, mental, emotional, and spiritual pain that disability inflicts on an individual. However, it is not necessary for a person with a physical disability to work through all of the accumulated layers of pain and heartache, to excavate, analyze and try to resolve all of the emotional turmoil in order to treat the people around them with love, kindness and respect. A person with a disability can release the burden from their heart and the poison from their spirit by going to the Cross of Jesus Christ and committing their past, present, and future to Jesus. After that, the disability, the pain, and the resentment will still try to speak but the urgent whispers of the Holy Spirit saying, "'Be ye kind one to another' is the law of God" will be louder. Over time, those urgent whispers will drown out self-pity and self-centeredness.

Love

For the marriage partner who has reached the end of their rope and is in the bedroom packing their bags because they cannot take one more moment, there is a last refuge and hope. Love is a choice and a decision, but it is also something else. The love of God which indwells all born-again believers is also an empowerment. Often spouses embittered by living with the pressures of physical disability need to read 1 Corinthians 13:1-8.which describes the nature of the love that is within them. As they read, they need to ask God to let His love rise up in their hearts and renew their strength and ability to love their partner and keep their vows.

Practical Strategies that Relieve Everyday Pressures

There are some practical strategies that a couple can use to ease some of the pressures in their everyday life. Using these strategies will whittle the obnoxious, obscene, and overbearing bully of disability down to size and minimize its influence on a marriage.

Develop a Life-Management Network

A life-management network is a practical strategy that has a dual purpose. In the case of a marriage where a husband has a disability but is able to communicate, this strategy allows the husband to fulfill his leadership role and at the same time take some of the responsibilities off of his wife's shoulders. He does this by organizing a network of people who can help take care of the things in life that need to be done which he cannot physically do. It also may involve finding alternate ways to provide for his physical care either on a regular or respite basis. He finds people he can activate with a simple phone call or e-mail to maintain the lawn, handle minor home repairs, auto maintenance, tax issues and any other thing he would typically handle himself. He can also add backup caregivers and alternative ways of transporting himself around town to this network. If his wife works, he may even want to add a part-time housekeeper. This network can become very creative and may require some good communication and negotiations between the husband and wife to find out exactly what arrangements would give her the help she wants and needs.

This kind of the system relieves the pressure on the wife and empowers the husband. It also helps relieve role reversal stress. Through the network system, the husband builds his leadership skills and carries out his responsibilities. No one feels overwhelmed. No one feels voiceless. No one abdicates. Life management networking takes a proactive approach to problem solving and keeps procrastination under control.

Having responsibilities distributed through a network insures that faithful friends do not become victims of helper burnout.

Exercise Independence

Spouses with a disability must begin to actively exercise independence in order to take their life back. They need to do everything possible to reclaim what disability has stolen. Exercising independence neutralizes the influence of disability on marriage and relieves marital stress. Stress is a marriage killer. People with disabilities need to have hobbies because hobbies relieve stress. They also need to get outside and exercise in fresh air for the same reason. If at all possible, they need to get out into the community on their own at various times to increase their independence from their spouse. The benefits of doing this are extraordinary. It helps them to gain poise, confidence, and physical strength, learn practical problem solving and have a renewed sense of being back in the game.

This writer has always tried to be as independent as possible as he lives with his quadriplegia. However, he has sometimes gotten stuck at a certain level without realizing it, and it took the courage of a close friend to point this out. After that, I made a habit of getting out at least once a month to get a haircut, go to lunch alone, and/or attend to other chores downtown. Over time, I became so independent that I could take myself to the doctor, go to the grocery store, and even do laundry at the Laundromat. When my wife had surgery unexpectedly, I was able to step up to the plate and take charge.

Regaining independence relieved pressure on my marriage and other relationships. Routinely getting out on my own gave me a sense of normalcy that I had lost. It wasn't my old normal life, but it didn't have to be. By getting out on my own in the chair, I was actually leaving the grieving I had been doing for my old life and healthy body. After fifteen years, I finally left the funeral and embraced life as it is today. It gave me a new sense of normalcy. The point is I didn't do any of these mental and the emotional exercises consciously; it happened automatically when I decided to go out to breakfast and get a haircut.

Relearning daily routines also increases personal independence and relieves stress on a marriage. Cooking, cleaning, washing dishes, vacuuming, and doing other chores enhance self-image and relieve pressure on the working spouse. It also may help to develop intimacy. Dr. Kevin Lehman, a Christian author, has written a book for married couples entitled *Sex Begins in the Kitchen*. In this book, he discusses the relationship between marital intimacy and being connected to the whole marriage including daily household tasks. There are two keys to making this connection work. First of all, helping is received much better when it comes from a loving heart that has no ulterior motives. Secondly, it has to be done in conjunction with a life management network strategy designed to help eliminate exhaustion. The bottom line is that the more a person with a disability develops their independence, the more joy they will get out of life on all levels.

Develop an Active Social Life

Studies show that having fun and doing things with friends is one of the most vital elements in a marriage that is going to survive the impact of physical disability. *Couples impacted by physical disability have a tendency to withdraw and become reclusive. They get so wrapped up in their own world and so preoccupied with feeding their live-in bully that they don't get out much.* There are also fear and logistical issues that keep them close to home. It is absolutely essential that they get out, have fun, and get involved with other people as much as they possibly can.

An active social life and interaction with others will help put the color back in the rainbow and the sun back in the sky. There are literally no boundaries to the activities in which a couple can participate. Almost any disability can be compensated for if they are simply willing to try. Church groups, Christian camps, and retreat programs for people with disabilities offer invaluable helps for couples desiring to re-energize their social and recreational life. The encouragement and safety net these groups provide when the unexpected occurs makes it easier for couples with disabilities to start becoming more active. They can also help a couple renew and reinforce their spiritual life.

A couple's social and recreational life can be as broad as their interests and imagination. They should try to have one date together every week and do something with other couples twice a month. They don't have to spend a lot of money. The idea is to have fun and relax. Once couples take the admittedly scary step of getting out and going places, they find many destinations and recreational attractions go out of their way to accommodate people with disabilities. They often get preferred front row seating at concerts and shows for the price of regular reserved seating. Theme parks and other attractions frequently offer reduced rates and special assistance for patrons with physical disabilities. Sometimes they are even invited to go to the head of the line eliminating long waits for popular attractions.

Develop a Spiritual and Emotional Support Network

Most couples, regardless of their circumstances, need structures and people in their lives who will give them the spiritual and emotional underpinning they need to withstand the pressures of life. Each partner will also need individual support. Becoming active in a Bible-believing church is a good place to start. In addition to camp and retreat programs, disability ministries offer chapter support groups in certain areas as well as Internet support groups. While involvement in these kinds of groups is often initially painful and difficult, it is vital because it allows couples to vent their feelings and frustrations to others who have been through, or who are in the process of going through, the same experiences.

Each partner in the marriage relationship should try to find someone who can be a sounding board and a prayer/accountability partner. An accountability partnership is a two-way relationship based on mutual honesty, transparency, and absolute confidentiality. It is often easiest to start an accountability partnership between two same-sex Christians who do not know one another very well. It is often easier to admit failures, failing, and unflattering truths to someone who starts out as a virtual stranger.

It can also be tremendously helpful to have a close-knit circle of friends who stay in touch through e-mail or frequent phone calls. They can also function as a personal prayer circle that can provide spiritual support and wisdom.

One of the tendencies in families impacted by disability is to "circle the wagons" and keep the outside world at a distance. They need to break through that defensive mindset and establish connections with friends. Friends will not only offer honesty and support, they provide opportunities for the couple to reciprocate and give from their own heart.

Schedule Respite Times

If a spouse is serving as a primary caregiver, they should schedule periodic respite times where they can get completely away from caregiving and having to deal with the world of disability. *The hardest thing for a spouse/caregiver to do is to separate the person they love most in the world from the disability that wreaks so much chaos in their lives.* Taking a total break from caregiving allows them to recalibrate their mind, spirit, and emotions in order to see the qualities they love about the person apart and distinct from the disability.

The frequency and length of respite times depends on the individual situation. Some people need 24 consecutive hours once or twice a month; others need one week twice a year. It may even take some trial and error to figure out how much time is needed, but periodic respite is good for both partners. It allows the caregiving spouse to recharge their batteries and helps the partner with a disability to fully appreciate the love and energy the caregiving partner invests in them and their relationship.

The most difficult aspect of scheduling respite times is finding competent and trustworthy people to act as caregivers. If the caregiving spouse takes time off but has to worry about their loved one the entire time they're gone, it isn't worth taking the time off. If they have to clean up messes that were not taken care of properly, redo procedures that weren't done correctly, or calm a traumatized husband, it is not worth going away.

The local church should not be afraid to step up and help with respite care. Learning to care for a person with a physical disability is not difficult but it has to be done thoroughly, correctly and compassionately.

"Invest Your Life in Something Larger Than Yourself!"

When pastor, evangelist, and former Bible college chancellor, Lowell Lundstrom and his wife Connie were asked about the secret of their youthfulness, energy, success, and sense of excitement, they replied, "Invest your life in something larger than yourself!" People impacted by physical disability have to be careful that they do not allow themselves to become the center of their universe or the biggest people in their own world. Often a natural pattern develops in the life of a couple dealing with disability. Because they are always dealing with their issues, they are always on the receiving end of kindness. As their relationship grows stronger and their ability to cope with their situation increases, they need to look beyond their own wants, needs, problems, and craziness to see the needs of others in the outside world. As they become involved in meeting the needs of other people, they will find tremendous happiness and joy in being a blessing and a channel that God can use. When they focus on a world that is centered on others rather than themselves, they develop new perspectives on their own situation, new attitudes, new priorities, and a new sense of balance in life.

A Word to the Wise

Marriage is not a proposal that can be taken lightly. Not everyone is able to handle the pressures in a marriage impacted by physical disability. There have been Christian men and women who have found that they just could not take any more. As a result, they did everything they could to get their spouse to hate them and the situation; they made their world a living hell just so they could get out of the marriage.

Even though there are winning strategies for marital success, proven methods of negotiation and communication that work, and God-given biblical principles which can turn impossible situations around, there are still some couples who absolutely should never get married in the first place.

The Joyful Side of Christian Marriage Impacted by Physical Disability

To some, it may seem as though a marriage touched by disability is an utterly and completely miserable thing. Nothing could be further from the truth. When two people are committed to Jesus Christ and to one another, their marriage can be filled with happiness, joy, and satisfaction in spite of difficulties that may arise or the challenges of living with physical disability. Here are some of the specific areas in which living with physical disability can enhance life experiences and bring joy into a marriage.

Transparent Communication

After dealing with one issue after another, and continually being transparent with one another, couples living with physical disability can reach an extraordinary level of closeness over time that may not have been possible if they didn't have to fight for their relationship. When one marriage partner begins to fight for their relationship, he or she refuses to let the other partner hide anger, resentment, or grief. It means the couple engages in a lifelong dialogue that may take occasional timeouts, but it is never silent for long. There is security in the knowledge that a husband and wife share a mutual conviction that love endures and life continues - even in the face of brokenness and loss. There is comfort in the knowledge that love can surpass and overtake shattered expectations and physical dysfunction.

Compassionate, Open-minded Children

Kids raised around people with disabilities accept and tolerate people who are different. They show tremendous compassion, demonstrate a willingness to serve, and are not intimidated by either the conditions others have or the various types of hardware and equipment they need.

Unique Circle of Friends

The Christian world and the world of disability bring together unique friends who share a precious faith and difficult experiences.

They are able to support one another, love each other in spite of faults and failings, and face adversity with faith and humor. Having such friends underscores the value of being a part of a Bible-believing church and getting involved in camps, retreats, support groups, and other programs sponsored by ministries to people with disabilities.

Unique Experiences

Overcoming the challenges presented by disability, and doing it together, makes the experiences of life and the marriage relationship sweeter and more precious. Couples living life in the face of physical disability are continually reclaiming lost ground and exploring new frontiers. Whether it's crossing the street in a wheelchair, going down a river in a canoe, watching stock car races from trackside because the wheelchair doesn't fit in the bleachers, or flying for the first time, every day offers new opportunities to push back the influence of disability and grow closer together as a couple and family.

HOW THE LOCAL CHURCH CAN MINISTER TO FAMILIES IMPACTED BY PHYSICAL DISABILITY

Here are five simple things the local church can do which will make an eternal difference in the life of a family that deals with physical disability.

Reach out, Reach out, and Reach out Again!

Churches with disability ministries need to understand that couples who live in the world of physical disability, and especially those who are new to it, can be withdrawn, reclusive and self-absorbed. They are so hunkered down in their own bunker and wrapped up in their own world that they can't see anything or anyone else. They are often unaware of their own neediness.

Church ministry groups and individual Christians need to reach out, and continue to reach out, until they get a positive response. Sometimes people in this kind of situation don't respond positively at first to those who reach out because of past experiences they have had with others who didn't follow through. *Sometimes people with disabilities are looking for consistency and reality because they have been victimized by those who only want to win a merit badge in social do-gooding. Once their project is completed, the merit badge secured, and the warm fuzzy feeling and glow has been experienced, they disappear, and the families with disabilities and other real problems are left to carry on alone.*

Consistency, patience, and follow-through will help build a quality disability ministry with a reputation for compassion and integrity. This should be the goal of every congregation.

Help Couples Achieve Spiritual Stability and Consistency

The daily stress of dealing with the challenges of physical disability can create a roller coaster effect on the spiritual lives of the people involved. Sunday school classes, small-group Bible studies, prayer retreats, conferences, and other activities will help couples struggling with a physical disability become spiritually grounded and realize that the physical disability is only a small component of their life. Seeing life from the eternal perspective reduces the influence and impact of disability on a marriage and family.

Help Couples Find and Develop Their Spiritual and Ministry Gifts

It is absolutely essential that people coping with physical disability have opportunities to discover their areas of giftedness and their place of ministry in the body of Christ. Couples impacted by physical disability receive many things from others all of the time. They are looking for ways in which they can give back and bless others. It is imperative to understand that a disability, no matter how profound, never disqualifies anyone from having a place in the body of Christ where they can exercise a God-given gift and fulfill their God-given call to minister.

Help Couples Become a Part of the Social and Recreational Life of the Church

One of the greatest steps a couple confronting physical disability can take is when they decide that nothing is going to keep them from enjoying life and being involved in their favorite sports and recreation. It may take some coaxing, but a group of friends within the church such as a young couples group can be the key in getting them started.

With the equipment and resources available today, there is no legitimate reason why a person with a physical disability and their family cannot have a full recreational life.

Assist with Practical Ministry Help When Needed

Periodically these couples and their families may need some practical assistance. Newlyweds might need help to set their house in order. They may need assistance in building access ramps or help getting their life management network together. If they are new to the community or to the state, they will need help getting connected to government and community programs that assist people with disabilities. They may also need financial counseling and help setting up a monthly budget.

The church can also help out during emergencies. There may be times when the spouse with a disability may be shut-in for medical reasons. People from the church should visit periodically and see if they can help in any way. There also will be times when the caregiving spouse falls ill, has to have surgery, or must be absent for some reason. These are times when the church can offer valuable help with light housekeeping, meals, respite care, and transportation.

Practical ministry or the meeting of "felt needs" can be a key to opening the door to a spiritual discussion and the presentation of Jesus Christ as the ultimate answer to every person's need or spiritual peace and reconciliation with God. If a church congregation will do these five things with open hands and hearts, it will provide couples and families dealing with physical disability a soft place to land.

Never-Never Land

On the other hand, there are several things that a Christian friend or a church disability ministry should never, ever do!

Never Take Sides

Always rally around the *couple*. Never take sides. That is divisive. It reinforces the disagreement and fuels division rather than resolution. Taking sides can become epidemic. It can split a ministry team and/or the church. Relationships of any kind, especially Christian relationships, should never be about being right or winning. They are about standing side-by-side, hand-in-hand, heart-to-heart to shine for Jesus in a world that is unaware of the love of God. Christian marriage is not about being right. Speaking about marriage in general, one man asked, "Do you want to be married or do you want to be right?"

Never Make Judgments or Assumptions

Sometimes people outside a relationship will see things happen in lives and marriages that cause them to raise an eyebrow and become concerned. Concern is good; assumptions are bad. It is very dangerous for Christian friends and supporters of a couple impacted by physical disability to make judgments or assumptions about circumstances, situations and feelings within the marriage. While God sees the inner workings and the deepest thoughts of hurting, broken hearts, outsiders, no matter how well-intentioned do not have the right to condemn a caregiving spouse. It is totally out of line to say things like, "Your spouse doesn't love you. If they did, they wouldn't treat you this way or take care of you this way."

If a friend or ministry group has concerns or opinions of this nature, they need to reserve them for the privacy and sanctity of their prayer closet. Making such condemnations and accusations to anyone but Jesus is irresponsible and unacceptable. The caregiving partner may have physical, mental, emotional or spiritual factors in their life that are making it difficult or impossible for them to provide quality care. It may have absolutely nothing to do with whether or not they love their spouse who is living with a disability.

Never forget or underestimate the fact that it is the relentless nature of physical disability to overwhelm and wear out those who are intimately impacted by it. Outsiders should never forget that for all of their good works, good hearts, and good intentions, at the end of the day, most of them go home and leave the disability behind. Couples impacted by physical disability can never leave it behind. One way or another, it becomes part of their life 24/7/365. Remember the premise with which this chapter began. Because a couple is "one flesh," the impact of physical disability is not limited to the partner who was diagnosed with the disability.

Never Give up on a Couple or Their Marriage

Always fight *for* the couple and never against them. The concept of "one flesh" is not biblical poetry; is a biological and spiritual reality that God takes very seriously. God doesn't take divorce casually and neither should Christian friends or the local church. It is absolutely unacceptable for friends or supporters to express the notion that if one partner leaves, it would be no big deal, it wouldn't be the worst thing that could happen, or that it would be for the best in the long run. Taking this kind of position shows a cold indifference and reflects a worldly, unbiblical view of marriage. It also demonstrates ignorance of principles of spiritual warfare. Marital conflict is not about personalities or overwhelming circumstances; it is a spiritual attack by a spiritual enemy. Advocating or being indifferent to divorce when disability issues are involved is surrendering to the enemy without a fight. These opinions are totally unacceptable among those who are part of a ministry designed to reach out to people with disabilities among whom marital difficulties are common.

This entire chapter boils down to the truth that a couple impacted by physical disability is fighting for the survival of their relationship on many fronts. There are physical, psychological, emotional and spiritual aspects of this battle. If Christian friends and disability ministries will make it their mission to support them with prayer, surround them with love, and serve them by washing their feet, these couples will have a better than fighting chance to survive and thrive while living from day-to-day with physical disability.

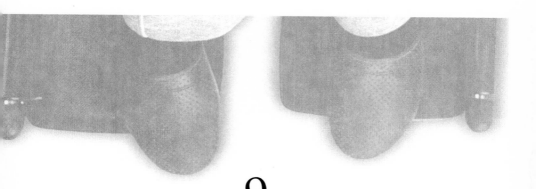

9.

Finding Their Place in the Body: The Ministry of People with Disabilities in the Church

OBJECTIVES

- ☐ To understand the ultimate goal of ministry to people with disabilities.

- ☐ To develop a vision for helping people with disabilities find their place in the body of Christ.

- ☐ To understand the six responses to suffering.

- ☐ To explore ways of providing people with disabilities the opportunities they need to develop their ministry gifts.

THE CONCEPT

Every believer in Jesus Christ, regardless of whether or not they have a disability, has God-given gifts and talents and a place in the body of Christ where those gifts and talents can be used to bless the family of God and minister to the world.

Foundation Scriptures

Ephesians 4:11-12, 16; 1 Cor. 12

Introduction

Reaching people with the gospel is actually a three-part process that consists of: evangelism, discipleship and ministry. Ministry to people with disabilities and the ministry of people with disabilities are interconnected and interdependent. Every church which seeks to evangelize the community of people with disabilities also has to have a vision for discipling or training them and helping them to find their place of giftedness and service once they have encountered Christ.

The purpose of discipleship is equipping the saints to minister. Scripture teaches that every member of the body, regardless of whether or not they live with a disability, is essential to the well-being of the whole:

> *From Him the whole body, joined and held together by every supporting ligament, grows and builds itself up in love, as each part does its work.* Eph. 4:16 (NIV)

The ultimate goal of ministry to people with disabilities is to help them to find their place of ministry in the body of Christ and to help them develop their ministry gifts. This is the natural result of evangelizing and discipling people with disabilities. Unfortunately, many ministries to people with disabilities lose their focus and spend all their time, energy, and resources meeting needs for the sake of meeting needs.

Once people with disabilities come into the church and have an encounter with Christ, a church may think its job is done. Sometimes when pastors and congregations look at the people with disabilities in their midst, they see only the problems and limitations. They don't realize everyone has God-given gifts which God expects to be used in the body of Christ to bless the congregation, the community and the world. *If people with disabilities in the local church aren't ministering, or being trained to minister, the ministry of the church as a whole is disabled, and the maturity of the church is retarded in the truest sense of the word.*

People with disabilities are far more than the sum of their problems and limitations.

Jesus taught His disciples that giving, as well as receiving, was to be a part of the Christian experience. Because of the nature of disability, people with disabilities tend to get stuck in a receiving rut. This usually happens because:

1. Other people believe the person with a disability is incapable of ministering to others.

2. The person with a disability believes he is incapable of ministering to others.

3. Opportunities to minister to others are not being identified and/or provided for the person with a disability.

4. The person with a disability does not take the opportunity to minister to others.

In order to see people with disabilities become fully-functioning, contributing, ministering members of the body, the local church must have a biblical vision and provide opportunities for ministry.

Having a Biblical Vision

Biblical Perception: Viewing Disability the Way God Does

As churches reach out to people with disabilities and bring them into their congregations, it is important for them to view disability the way God does. The Bible makes it very clear that people with disabilities are not victims, casualties, or accidents that have taken God by surprise:

> *The LORD said to him [Moses], "Who gave man his mouth? Who makes him deaf or mute? Who gives him sight or makes him blind? Is it not I, the LORD? Now go, and I will help you speak and teach you what to say."* (Ex. 4:11)

There is a lot of debate among theologians, those involved in disability ministry, and the community of people with disabilities as to the extent which God actually deliberately creates people with disabilities; however, this passage makes it very clear that God is not afraid to take responsibility for His creation. In Exodus 4, God commissions Moses to set His people free, and He makes several important points that are relevant to the ministry rendered by people with disabilities in the local church:

- □ Disability and weakness does not disqualify believers from being called by God to do great things.

- □ Disability and weakness are not justifiable excuses for not responding to God's call.

- □ God promises to compensate for disabilities and weaknesses and to support, teach and empower those who answer His call.

Other passages tell us that:

- □ God has a purpose and plan for every life even if they are in some sort of confinement or captivity (Jer. 29:11).

- □ People with disabilities are often "miracles in the making." They have a special destiny, and are waiting for a divine appointment (John 9:3).

- □ All believers, including those with disabilities, have been given gifts they can use to bless others (1 Cor. 12:11; Rom. 12:4-6a).

- □ Personal weakness or disability is an asset to ministry if God is going to get the glory. People with disabilities are acutely aware of their weaknesses, and they understand the necessity of having an empowerment that comes from God (1 Cor. 1:27-29; 2 Cor. 12:9-10).

After the leadership and those involved in disability outreach in the local church are able to see people with disabilities the way God does, they need to communicate their vision to the rest of the congregation. Once they get a vision for the aggressive evangelism of people with disabilities and those who are disenfranchised, they need to cast that vision so the congregation can prepare emotionally and spiritually to welcome these people groups into the family of God.

Education: Communicating the Vision to the Body

In seminars to teenagers on disability awareness, this writer makes the following analogy:

Once there was a survey in which teenagers were asked how they felt about themselves. The majority of respondents said they felt ugly, unloved, and misunderstood. Coincidently, I often have those same feelings. When I became a quadriplegic I began to notice certain similarities between having a disability and being a teenager. As a teenager, I often thought that I looked weird, acted weird, and smelled weird. There are days I feel the same way as I live with this disability. Then there are other days when I just feel that other people see me as looking weird, acting weird and smelling weird.

There is an ugly and uncomfortable side to life with disability that has to be acknowledged and confronted. The world of disability can be filled with disfigurement, deformity, and muscular atrophy. The first day that I was rolled into a physical therapy gymnasium and saw quadriplegics, stroke victims, head trauma victims and amputees, I thought I was in a body and fender shop for human beings. It can be a very stinky, slimy, messy, noisy world where lots of rubber gloves and a good sense of humor are absolute necessities. The first time I went to a camp for people with disabilities, I thought they were having a food fight at lunch, but it was just a bunch of people with disabilities trying to eat. By the same token, in the early days of my own quadriplegia, my disability turned meals into obstacle courses that often made fellow diners uncomfortable. One day, I finally looked up at a friend of mine who was very embarrassed and uncomfortable as he watched me wrestle with my Jell-O and said, "Don't worry about me. I'm just a one-man food fight looking for a place to happen."

In the world of disability ministry, there are two types of churches. The first consists of congregations in which disability ministry is an isolated outreach that involves just a few members who are very passionate about their ministry. In these situations, the church at large may be fearful or intimidated by disabilities or differences. They may actually be revolted or repulsed by the messy, smelly, noisy, sometimes ugly side of disability. Many people choose to keep their distance from those who have physical, mental, or social challenges, and they need to get past the external factors that alienate them from people with disabilities. In the second type of church, reaching out to disenfranchised people is embraced by every person in every pew. In these churches, love and acceptance for people who are different or downtrodden is pervasive throughout the congregation.

When confronted with the ugly realities of disability, many people want to retreat to the safety of their comfort zone. They can be drawn out of their comfort zone in the following ways:

☐ Exposure: Dr. Phil McGraw says, "Monsters live in the dark." People are only intimidated by those things they don't understand. Interaction between people with disabilities and the congregation at large can begin the process of friendship evangelism and break down the barriers of prejudice and preconceptions on both sides. Some churches accomplish this by having a fellowship meal once a month where people with disabilities are the special guests.

☐ Recognize generational barriers: Many older people may not be ready to accept the new visibility, adaptability, and opportunities for interaction and ministry that are available to people with disabilities in today's society. This barrier can be bridged by exposing the older generation to the giftedness of people with disabilities. This can be done by booking a speaker or singer with a disability or by having a special-needs Sunday School class minister in the regular Sunday morning service.

☐ Involvement: The best education and exposure is hands-on foot washing. Taking a cross-section of the congregation on a disability-ministry missions trip to work at events such as a

Special Touch Summer Get Away, a Special Gathering retreat, or a camp at a place like Inspiration Center or Camp Daniel can dynamically change the perception, vision, direction, and the impact of a local church.

Discipleship: Communicating the Vision to People with Disabilities

If congregations at large have difficulty getting past some of the *external* ugliness of disability, people with disabilities often struggle with their *internal* feelings of being "ugly, unloved, and misunderstood" as well as their belief that their disability disqualifies them from ministering and being a blessing to other people. They need to reprogram their inner voice that has convinced them that they are no good, broken down, "on the shelf," and unable to participate in God's good plan.

COMMON RESPONSES TO SUFFERING

People with disabilities often cope with their disability by choosing one of five common responses to suffering.

The Pursuit of Pleasure

Hedonism is the pursuit of pleasure for its own sake. The hedonist says: "I don't deserve all of this pain and suffering. The world owes me. From now on I am going after all of the pleasure I can get." The hedonist is ruled by the Principle of Compensation. He or she wants relief though gluttony, sex, accumulation, and/or moral apathy.

Conquering Disability through Will-power

This approach can be summed up in the word, "Humanism." In the world of disability, humanists are those who are so neurotically independent that they cannot accept help from anyone - God or man. The humanist says: "I can beat this thing through the power of my own will!" The humanist lives by the Principle of Control and Conquest and employs science, social action, and/or guts and determination.

Escape

Escapism is emotional anesthesia. The escapist submerges himself, in a prolonged and unhealthy way, in fantasy worlds through all forms of entertainment or drugs in order to get away from the pain, problems and limitations of reality. The escapist says: "If I can't fix it at least I can ignore its effects on my life." The escapist lives by the principle of Capitulation and totally surrenders to those areas in their life they find are overwhelming them.

The Pursuit of Wealth and Stuff

Some people with disabilities fall into a life of materialism. They compensate for their pain and problems by anesthetizing themselves economically. A minority get started on this path when they receive extremely large insurance settlements that can range into the millions. The materialist says: "If I can't fix my disability, at least I can be comfortable." The materialist lives by a modified principle of Capitulation, Capitulation through Capitalism.

Faith in Anything but Jesus Christ

Religion seeks to make peace with suffering through believing in anything but Christ. It can revolve around any messianic figure from Elvis, to Maitreya (the New Age messiah), or Satan. Apart from Christ, religion results in bondage. You are strapped to the wreckage of an oncoming eternal disaster. The religionist says: "I can transcend it"

A "religionist" is simply a person with misplaced faith. They actually live by the very sound principle of Connection and Communion because they believe in something higher than themselves. But because the connection and communion is not with the Lord God Jehovah and His Only Son Jesus Christ, the religionist is holding on to nothing but an air castle that has no substance and is digging a well that holds no water.

Solomon experimented with all five of these false solutions and found them unsatisfactory. The book of Ecclesiastes documents his journey. His conclusion after a lifetime of self-indulgence was that everything apart from living in right relationship to God is meaningless. An individual living with a disability who chooses to cope through any of these false solutions needs either evangelism or discipleship.

Faith in Jesus Christ: The Biblical Response to Suffering

The Biblical response to suffering is true faith in the Lord Jesus Christ. The believer in Jesus Christ says: "I have the Person; I live in His Presence; I have His Power and His Peace, He gives me Purpose."

I can do all things through Christ which strengtheneth me. Phil. 4:13 (KJV)

Keep your lives free from the love of money and be content with what you have, because God has said, "Never will I leave you; never will I forsake you." (Heb. 13:5)

You did not choose me, but I chose you and appointed you to go and bear fruit--fruit that will last. . . (John 15:16)

The Christian lives by the principle of Connection and Communion with the Lord Jesus Christ.

People with disabilities cannot find their place in the world, their purpose in life, or the power to fulfill it until they stop pursuing dead-end paths that lead to heartbreak. Only a relationship with God through faith in Jesus Christ can provide ultimate fulfillment.

PROVIDING OPPORTUNITY

It is possible for people with disabilities to minister in any and every capacity in the church. However, not every person is right for every ministry. Sometimes all people need is time and training. Do not be afraid of trial and error and remember the truism, "practice makes perfect."

The most important thing to remember regarding the ministry of all believers is something that the late Pastor James Gast often told a young man in his congregation whose dream of going into the ministry had been derailed by a near-fatal car accident, "As long as a person draws breath in this world, God has a purpose for their life." It is up to the church to provide opportunities for those who have been derailed or are living with disability and other challenges. They need help and encouragement to fine-tune their God-given call and develop their ministry gifts. Remember, when providing opportunities for ministry development, you must be sensitive, creative, and flexible.

"As long as a person draws breath in this world, God has a purpose for their life."
– Pastor James Gast

Sensitivity

There are several areas in which the church needs to be sensitive as it seeks to develop the ministry of people with disabilities.

Be sensitive to the fact that the ministry of many people with disabilities may be silent. It may seem to be invisible and/or nonexistent, but regardless of their incapacity, people with severe and profound disabilities are still capable of touching the hearts and spirits of others. Angie Christiansen is a wonderful example of this fact. Angie was physically abused as an infant and suffered a brain injury. She is unable to walk or speak, but she has a delightful smile and a wonderful laugh. Angie was eventually adopted by a family who over the years have adopted many, many special-needs children. When Angie was four years old, her family attended the Special Touch Summer Get Away in Waupaca, Wisconsin. Angie's mother met a young woman who was totally overwhelmed with being the spouse and caregiver of a quadriplegic. The young woman took Angie on a pontoon boat ride, and while they rode back and forth across the lake, Angie's smile and laugh healed the young woman's hurt.

A church needs to be sensitive to the fact that God calls people to minister in spite of the fact that they have a disability. When God called Moses, he chose a man with a speech impediment to be His communicator and the leader of His chosen people. When Moses tried to beg off, God would not accept no for an answer. Therefore, a church should not disqualify a person from a ministry due to an "obvious" disability. Moses' case teaches us that just because a person has difficulty speaking, it doesn't mean he isn't called to be an exhorter, encourager, or a leader.

Rick and Dan attended the Special Touch Summer Get Away in Illinois. Both of them have moderate to severe cerebral palsy, and they have difficulty speaking. At the very end of a care and share time, the person in charge of the session made a comment about healing. Dan suddenly became angry and upset. He began to yell incoherently, and his anger caused him to have violent spasms. The group leaders felt totally overwhelmed and powerless. They had no idea what they should do or say. Rick came to the rescue. With the help of his caregiver and a language board, Rick began to quietly minister to Dan. After a while, Dan became quiet and thoughtful. That evening during the chapel service, Dan gave his heart to the Lord because Rick opened the way earlier that day.

Put people with disabilities into ministry situations and promote them as they grow in grace, knowledge, and their gift. Be sensitive to the Spirit in regards to those God may call to full-time ministry. People with disabilities in full-time ministry face tremendous obstacles as they strive to fulfill God's call on their life. It is often very difficult to find opportunities to prove to individuals in the non-disabled community that they are fully capable of ministering. People with disabilities who are in the ministry need to be encouraged emotionally, spiritually and financially.

Creativity

Creativity may have to be applied in overcoming the following obstacles which are common in ministry:

- ☐ Communication. These barriers may be overcome through the use of language boards, sign language and lip reading.

- ☐ Accessibility. These barriers may be overcome through the installation of ramps, wheelchair lifts, elevators, making spaces wider, and other types of accommodation. Areas that may need the attention include bathrooms, offices, sound rooms, choir lofts, and platform/pulpit areas.

- ☐ Strength and mobility: These barriers may be overcome through designating a personal assistant or attendant, the use of motorized wheelchair, van or bus, a van or bus service, and/ or accommodation depending on the individual's disability.

- ☐ Sensory limitations: Provide aids for the blind, the visually impaired and those in the deaf culture.

- ☐ Intellectual limitations: Provide ministry opportunities appropriate to the intellectual level, e.g. an intellectually appropriate chapel service.

- ☐ Transportation: Have discussions about transportation issues facing people with disabilities in the congregation, and then find creative ways to solve them.

Flexibility

One of the challenges facing full-time ministers with disabilities is the impact of the unpredictable nature of their disability on their ministry. Lay people with disabilities have the same challenges. Wheelchairs can tip over, involuntary bowel movements can occur, spasms and seizures can be disruptive, equipment can malfunction, and procedures can take longer than expected. The list of structure breakers and schedule stretchers is almost endless. Working with people with disabilities and accommodating their desire, obligation, and call to minister requires having a patient and flexible attitude with regard to time, schedules, and the built-in potential for crisis.

Detheatricalize the Worship Service

It is a given biblical standard that worship services need to be conducted "decently and in order," and certainly there should be an atmosphere of reverence. However, American worship services have often become scheduled and choreographed like theatrical productions that proceed without a hitch. Appearance has become extremely important. Everything has to look right and sound perfect. Everyone has to dress according to a particular standard or run the risk of disapproving looks, censure, ridicule and/or condemnation. Taken to an extreme, this can create a very intimidating environment for people with disabilities. This kind of environment can make it difficult for a person with a disability to show up, much less decide to invest time and energy to develop their areas of giftedness. The pastor and congregation must decide if their worship services are places where God's family gathers and everyone is accepted with the open arms of Jesus and ministry is encouraged, or if they are simply theatrical shows.

This can be somewhat difficult to evaluate. Here are some questions that will help you determine whether or not a congregation is completely ready for all aspects of ministry from people with disabilities:

□ Can the congregation appreciate the giftedness of a person with an intellectual disability even if they sing off key?

□ Can the congregation accept ministry from someone who preaches or shares a testimony from a wheelchair or with a speech impediment?

□ Can a congregation accept a delay in the service created by an usher who has a disability that slows them down or by a deacon or associate pastor who needs a moment to make adjustments during a communion service?

□ Is the congregation ready to accept a person with a disability praying for the sick?

Each pastor and congregation needs to make their own assessment and their own list of questions in order to determine how welcome people with disabilities really are to develop and use their ministry gifts.

Make Reasonable Schedules for Church Events

Sometimes people with disabilities are unable to participate in the life of the church simply because the starting time may be too early. In order for an average man to participate in a Saturday morning men's breakfast that begins at 7:00 AM, he will probably have to get up at 6:00 AM. A man with a disability may have to get up at 4:30 or 5:00 AM. Moving the event back a half-hour or an hour would help a person with a disability enormously without inconveniencing everyone else very much. Every individual congregation should be aware that time scheduling can be a factor as they can work out specific solutions for their particular church.

Count on Emergencies and Always Have a Back-up Plan

When working with people with disabilities, be proactive about unpredictability. If a singer with a disability is scheduled to perform special music, plan to have a back-up singer in case a problem arises, and they cannot appear. Ask all Sunday School teachers to submit an extra copy of their lesson plan so that a substitute can carry on if needed. If this is standard Sunday School policy, a teacher with a disability is covered in the event that unpredictability should raise its ugly head.

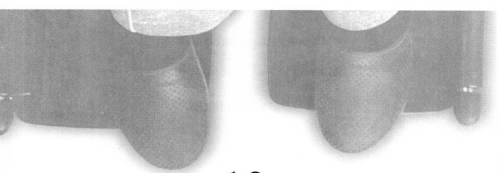

10.

Making the Cross Accessible: Ministering to the Blind and Visually Impaired

Objectives

- ☐ To understand the impact of vision loss.
- ☐ To develop sensitivity toward people with partial eyesight.
- ☐ To identify the essential elements of a church that is user friendly to the visually impaired.
- ☐ To learn how to welcome the blind and visually impaired into the church.
- ☐ To discover methods of making Sunday School accessible for blind children.

The Concept

The needs of the blind and visually impaired must be considered as the local church attempts to fully communicate to its congregation, community, and world that there is truly "room at the cross" for "whosoever will may come."

Foundation Scripture

Mark 16:15 (The Great Commission)

INTRODUCTION

Definitions

Legally Blind: A person is considered legally blind if their vision is less than 20/200 after correction of their better eye with single lens glasses or contacts, or if their field of vision is 20 degrees or less.

Visually Impaired: A person is considered visually impaired if normal activities in life are limited by a visual condition that is not correctable such as colorblindness, being unable to drive at night, or having dyslexia.

Statistics

Here are some important statistics about the blind that churches should consider as they design their ministry outreach programs:

- According to the 2000 Census, 1.3 million people in the United States are confirmed as legally blind.

- The American Foundation for the Blind estimated this number is actually about 4.5 million. The discrepancy exists because many estimates do not include individuals over 65, those who have multiple disabilities, and others who are not counted for various reasons.

- One out of ten people will be legally blind by the age of 65.

- One out of every thirty people has a severe visual impairment.

- According to the Lighthouse for the Blind, the figures given here will double by the year 2030. According to data released from the World Health Organization and Prevent Blindness America in 2002, these figures will double by the year 2020.

- There are 57,000 confirmed blind children in the United States and 448,000 who are severely visually impaired.

- ☐ Only about 10% of the blind have no vision at all.
- ☐ Only about 12% of the blind read Braille. This figure is up from 8% in 1994, but below the 38% recorded in 1964.
- ☐ Only about 35% of the blind use white canes, 2% use guide dogs and even *fewer* use human guides.

Why Are So Few Churches Attempting to Reach this Large Segment of the Population?

Leadership Is Unaware of the Need

- ☐ Church leaders may be unaware of what can be done. Usually just a few simple changes can make a big difference.
- ☐ Some are unaware of the need because the vision for this type of ministry has never been modeled or cast before them.
- ☐ Some may be apathetic, prejudiced, or confused about the priority of salvation vs. healing, or the value of providing evangelistic and ministry opportunities to the blind.

Some church leaders do not see the necessity for ministry to the blind and visually impaired because they do not see it as a part of the Great Commission as a whole.

The Blind Are Generally "Invisible"

- ☐ Very few blind people will have a cane or a dog.
- ☐ Most blind individuals either were familiar with their environment before they began losing their sight, or they learned to navigate proficiently within that environment after losing it.
- ☐ Eye contact is the primary means of establishing communication. Because of this, people may have difficulty in establishing a natural connection with the blind.

The Blind Tend to Blend

Blind individuals tend to prefer to blend in with the normal flow of the church. They make few demands for special accommodations.

Transportation Is Undependable

The lack of dependable transportation keeps the blind from participating in church services and activities.

THE IMPACT OF VISION LOSS

When a person is diagnosed with blindness or serious visual impairment, the effect can be devastating, not only to the individual but to their family as well.

The Psychological Impact

The medical determination that nothing more can be done to restore vision or prevent it from deteriorating further may lead one who has known sight to the conclusion that life itself is over. The emotions experienced around vision loss and blindness are deep and complex. Volunteers, friends, and family members may find that their desire and willingness to help and be supportive will not be enough to cope with the psychological and emotional trauma that a person with new sight-loss is experiencing. Pastoral or professional Christian counseling may be needed, and in serious situations, mental health and rehabilitation specialists may need to get involved.

Blindness is not just a nuisance like being left-handed in a right-handed world. It is not just an inconvenience like living in the suburbs and not being able to drive. . . . Blindness is, and I include severe vision impairment, a serious psychological, physiological, and cognitive blow to the individual, which, if left unattended, impedes and can even destroy any chance for a normal, productive life. - W. F. Gallagher, director of the American Foundation for the Blind.

The Social Impact

Some people fall into isolation and despair if they are unable to find acceptable solutions. Personal adjustment to vision loss does not occur in a social vacuum; it involves relationships with other people and the reactions of all concerned to the new situation. The inability to see and recognize familiar faces makes mingling and initiating conversations difficult. The pleasure of going to movies, plays, sports events, and other entertainment is diminished. The new circumstances change relationships. Misunderstandings erupt due to mistaken ideas, false impressions, or faulty perceptions on both sides of a relationship as people make blindness or other visual impairment a part of their life. This makes communication even more vital in maintaining healthy relationships.

Phases of Adjustment

Adjustment can be a lengthy process and while it is also very individual, certain phases can be identified. All phases do not occur in every case, nor do they occur in any specific order. *These phases, commonly referred to as the stages of grief, are typical of all cataclysmic disability experiences, not just blindness or visual impairment.*

Trauma

For the person whose vision has gradually worsened, devastating trauma may occur when the ophthalmologist says, "There is nothing more that can be done for your eyes." At that moment, important learned activities and tasks may seem to have become impossible.

Shock and Denial

People often feel stunned, numb, and unable to think. Denial may be expressed through the process of consulting a series of doctors in hopes of finding a cure. Others attempt to carry on as though there is no disability, rejecting opportunities for assistance in any form. The time it takes for an individual to adjust is based on how fast he or she is willing to accept the reality of the impairment.

Mourning and Withdrawal

A person experiencing vision loss may be withdrawn, isolated, self-centered, irritable, and may wallow in self-pity. This stage, like the previous one, is very difficult for friends and family. They need support and information about the help that is available. A good listener can also be of special value during this time.

Realization and Depression

The implications of vision loss are overwhelming. Feelings of loss, real or perceived, will set in as the individual confronts both the enormity and finality of what has happened. Those impacted by a traumatic loss of their sight or other disability often pass through a period marked by disbelief and the inability to accept the finality of what has happened. They postpone the acceptance of their new reality in the hope of a miracle, medical or otherwise.

Christians are especially liable to this kind of thinking, especially those who accept miracles as a major component of their theology. Indeed they have a reason for their confidence. They are not waiting; they are trusting in the Lord Jesus Christ. The Word of God very clearly states that Jesus Christ is the same yesterday, today, and forever. Miracles have not and will not pass away. Jesus regularly performs awesome miracles of healing. The problem is that they are not always within the time frame a Christian would prefer. Abraham waited twenty-five years for his miracle. The young man born blind in John chapter 9 waited his entire life for his miracle. The reality that a loving God might allow the person to live with the loss of their sight for many years can be deeply depressing.

Another complication is the mistaken belief that one can no longer do the things that gave him independence and a sense of enjoyment. Resistance and even hostility to the help of others may persist in the midst of continued emotional turmoil.

Reassessment and Reaffirmation

A new sense of identity begins to develop that includes vision impairment but is not centered on it. While a loss has indeed occurred, *everything* has not been lost. Eighty-five percent of people designated "legally blind" have usable vision. Emphasis on what is still possible is crucial during this phase in order to maintain hope and motivation. Goals for rehabilitation begin to be set.

Learning and Motivation

As limitations become more comfortable, self-consciousness emerges as new skills are learned. Accumulating successes builds confidence, but family and friends must be willing to accept and support the new found independence of the visually impaired person.

Self-acceptance and Self-esteem

Vision loss is accepted intellectually and emotionally. There is full involvement in activities of interest.

These phases of adjustment (stages of grief) are essential transition stages for every person who experiences a major trauma or loss regardless of its nature. The doctors at Sister Kinney Institute estimate that it takes at least 1-5 years for a person to accept their disability.

Being Sensitive to People with Partial Eyesight

Often people with partial eyesight do not appear to be visually impaired. Although they may wear ordinary glasses, this does not mean their vision is corrected to 20/20. The following tips were adapted from information provided by The Assemblies of God National Center for the Blind.

- When you meet a visually-impaired person, always speak first and identify yourself, even if you are familiar with one another. Don't assume that your voice will be recognized.

- At a bus stop, if someone asks you for the number of an approaching bus, consider the possibility he or she doesn't see the bus number. Answer politely. Do the same in a store where price labels may be virtually illegible to a visually-impaired person.

☐ If you know someone who's losing eyesight, don't hesitate to ask, "Do you have difficulty seeing me?" Questions like this will break the ice. The loss of eyesight creates a tremendous deprivation. Opening the subject for discussion will help both you and the person living with the loss.

☐ If your friend is visually impaired, volunteer assistance. Asking for help is very difficult for most people. An offer such as, "May I help with your mail?" or "I'm on my way to the market; may I pick something up for you?" will be greatly appreciated.

☐ When walking with a partially-sighted person, identify the terrain, in your path. Mention curbs, cracked, uneven spots in the sidewalk, potholes in the street, and/or low-hanging tree branches. Allow the visually-impaired person to set the pace of the walk and take hold of your arm.

☐ When giving directions to a visually-impaired person, be explicit. Say something like, "The door is to your right." rather than "The door is over there."

☐ Continue to use phrases that refer to sight, e.g., "Did you watch that TV program?" or "How nice it is to see you." Ours is a visually oriented culture. Trying to avoid phrases like this can create unnecessary awkwardness. Don't be surprised when visually-impaired people continue to use these phrases.

☐ When writing to a visually impaired person, clarity is important. Don't jumble letters together. Printing is clearer than a cursive script. Use a black felt-tip pen on white paper. This often creates enough contrast to allow a partially-seeing person to read what you have written with or without assistance of visual aids.

☐ Don't "lump" disabilities together. Just because a person is partially-sighted, it does not mean the individual has other physical or intellectual disabilities. Be sensitive; don't be condescending.

☐ If spoken to by a visually impaired person, respond verbally. A nod or a smile might not be seen.

☐ If an elder is socially isolated and remains homebound, consider the possibility of vision loss. Impaired eyesight can and does reduce mobility.

THE ESSENTIAL ELEMENTS OF A BLIND-FRIENDLY CHURCH

Begin with Prayer

Prayerfully and carefully examine your motives, philosophy of ministry, theology, and attitudes toward the blind and visually impaired.

Locate the Blind in Your Community

Every effort must be made to take the gospel message to the blind because very few of them will be in your church. Almost all communities have some types of social organization for the blind. These can be found by contacting local libraries, the Lions Club, state vocational rehabilitation agencies, welfare agencies, the National Federation of the Blind, the American Council of the Blind, hospitals, as well as state and county health services for both the elderly and people with disabilities. Since ninety percent of the blind are seniors, nursing homes and senior organizations are also good resources. Make contact with the blind through these organizations and make them aware that you are a blind-friendly church.

Educate the Church

In order to establish an effective outreach to the blind and visually impaired, the whole church has to be involved. This means the entire church needs to understand the needs of individuals with visual impairments and what it will take to include them in the life of the church. Education begins with the leadership, but it involves everyone.

Make Communication Accessible

The gospel is only as accessible as the means used to communicate it. Using small print in a bulletin is like lighting a lamp and holding it under a bushel. Audible, large print, and Braille formats should be used in communication.

Help with Transportation

Inadequate transportation is probably the biggest hindrance to the blind, visually impaired, and others with disabilities who are interested in attending or becoming involved in a church. Very few communities have adequate affordable transportation for people with disabilities. Many who lose their vision when they are older may never have the mobility skills necessary to use public transportation.

Often churches will provide transportation only for the Sunday morning service. People who are blind, visually impaired, or have another form of disability are unable to attend men's fellowships, women's fellowships, youth activities, social gatherings, and other events that make up the life of the church. Until a person is involved and recognized as a part of the church family, asking for rides can be very awkward.

How much transportation a church will provide and how the congregation will be involved are key ministry decisions. The entire congregation must be made aware of the outreach's ministry and how individuals can get involved. Always keep transportation issues in mind when planning community-wide evangelical out-reaches.

Make Worship Accessible

Every effort should be made to offer alternatives to standard print or projected information. Bulletins, songs, and Sunday school material, etc. should be available in large print. Volunteers from the congregation can record information on cassettes, CD's, mp3 and/or other media. It's important that the entire congregation know what is available and that regular audible announcements are made.

Churches with a voice-mail system may want to record the bulletin and other special announcements and make it a numerical option on the church telephone line. This is a very important option for the blind and visually impaired, and it is appreciated by many in the congregation.

Make Facilities Accessible

The American Disabilities Act now requires that signs be posted in Braille. *However, only twelve percent of the blind read Braille. This means that ninety percent of the blind who enter a church will not be able to read the signs.* Signs with large contrasting letters can save a lot of potential embarrassment. Offering optional orientation to the facilities can make things easier. Often that will be all that is needed for a visually-impaired or blind person to move independently around the building. In fact, offering optional and facility orientation is a wonderful courtesy that should be available to all visitors. Facility orientation is one of those extra touches that can help make a visitor feel like they are a part of the church family.

Have a Friendly Congregation

There is no substitute for a friendly, caring congregation that is always ready to offer help when needed. Keeping the church family circle open, and helping newcomers find their place in the circle, is the mark of a friendly congregation.

Promote Involvement

Get the blind or visually-impaired person busy in the life of the congregation. All believers have something to give. Personal involvement is the best way to take ownership of a church and get to know the people. With ownership and involvement comes identity.

Make Accessible Resources Available

Many Christian resources are available to assist the blind and visually impaired. Bibles, Sunday School materials, reference books, and many other resources are available in Braille, large print, and in audio formats. However, sometimes extra diligence is needed to find them. Information on ministry resources for the blind can be obtained through organizations such as the Assemblies of God Center for the Blind, CARE Ministries Inc. (an interdenominational resource center), the National Library Service for the Blind, the American Foundation for the Blind, and Recordings for the Blind and Dyslexic.

WELCOMING THE BLIND AND VISUALLY IMPAIRED INTO THE CHURCH

Churches are often hesitant to begin outreaches to the blind and people with other disabilities because they lack training and knowledge. They fear venturing into an unknown area and making mistakes. Christians should never allow the fear of failure to keep them from taking first steps into a new area of ministry. Reassurance is found in 1 Cor. 13:8: *"Love never fails!"*

The following are some basic points of good etiquette that should be observed when interfacing with the blind or visually impaired. Every member of the pastoral staff, Christian Education staff, ushers, greeters, and the congregation should understand these do's and dont's.

Do's

☐ Go out of your way to speak to a visitor or member who may be blind or visually impaired. Always identify yourself by name. If it is the first time the person has attended your church, take a few minutes to get to know them and make them feel welcome.

☐ Let a person who is blind know that you are going to touch them before you do. You might say something like, "I'd like to shake your hand and welcome you to our church."

☐ Offer to show blind or visually-impaired visitors the location of restrooms, Sunday School rooms, the pastor's office, the church office, and the fellowship hall. You might also offer to take them around the sanctuary and point out where the baptistery, communion rail, altar, choir loft, and other features are located.

- ☐ Make sure to point out the availability of special resources that your church offers, such as large-print hymn books, audio tapes, etc.

- ☐ Permit them take your bended arm. This is known as a sighted-guide technique. After they take your arm, walk at comfortable pace slightly ahead of them. If you are going up or down stairs, or through a crowd or a door, just let them know. They will move slightly behind you. Ask them to help you adjust this technique to their individual needs. They will be glad to help you.

- ☐ Offer to help them sit down in a chair. Guide their hand to the back of the chair so they can gather knowledge about the chair before sitting down. It may be appropriate to provide verbal information about the chair's placement,

- ☐ Let them know how long they will be left alone if you must leave them in a strange place. Physical contact with a wall, chair, tree, etc. will help prevent them from becoming disoriented.

- ☐ Offer help to a person with a cane or guide dog. Even though they have assistance, they may still have difficulty finding their way around. If they prefer to follow you as you walk together, walk comfortably ahead of them, and let them know if you are getting ready to stop.

- ☐ Volunteer to pick them up for special events and church services. Many rely on public transportation, which is often not available in the evenings or on weekends when church activities normally take place. If you say you will be there at a specific time, be sure to show up! If you will be late, call and let them know. *Transportation is one of the main reasons persons who are blind, visually-impaired or have other disabilities do not attend church.*

- ☐ Advise a blind person with whom you have been talking if you are going to leave them. It can be very embarrassing to talk to someone who is not there.

- [ ] Regard them as fellow disciples of the Lord. Each person has ministry gifts and talents and may be able to contribute in very positive ways to the life and ministry of your church.

- [ ] Volunteer to read the church bulletin aloud or share information on bulletin boards and special signs so that they will know what is going on at the church.

- [ ] Give verbal feedback during conversations to let your blind or visually-impaired friends know that you are listening to them.

- [ ] Be patient. Recognize that they may eat more slowly, walk more slowly, and orientate themselves more slowly, etc.

- [ ] Be specific when describing the location of an object. Guide their hands so they can touch the object rather than pointing at it.

- [ ] Consider inviting them to your home or out for a meal. You will find a warm friendship that goes beyond any physical limitations if you just take the opportunity to provide fellowship. If you're uncomfortable or curious about something related to their vision loss, ask about it but don't make it the major thrust of your conversation. If it is a child who is blind, include them in the youth and children's activities, and make sure their parents feel welcome.

Don'ts

- [ ] Don't pet or feed a guide dog or other disability service dog without the owner's prior permission. These working dogs have mastered a fairly disciplined set of procedures and should always be considered "on duty." Distracting them by petting or playing with them may create safety concerns for the person who is blind. These dogs are legally able to go anywhere the person goes, including restaurants and churches. If your services are long, you might need to identify an out-of-the-way grassy place as a dog relief area. Ushers should be prepared to assist those using service dogs to get to these areas.

☐ Don't pull or push a blind or visually impaired person when you are assisting them.

☐ Don't focus on a person's blindness or other disability, or insist that God would heal them if they just had enough faith. Those who are blind may still be dealing with spiritual issues concerning their loss of vision, and they may be uncomfortable discussing it with people who do not love and accept them as they are. There is no way that you can know what is going on in an individual's heart so never make automatic spiritual assumptions. People have a tendency to assume that someone who is blind or has another physical disability either does not have enough faith to be healed or is being judged because of sin. The individual with the disability may simply be following the scriptural admonition in Ephesians 6:13, 14 which says, *"having done all to stand. Stand..."* In other words, they have a heart that is full of faith and have fully committed the matter to God; they are waiting for their healing. They understand God is in complete control of their situation.

☐ Don't let a person's blindness or other disability intimidate you into treating them as if they were invisible. Invite them to sit with you, and/or offer to help them find someone they know.

☐ Don't assume that every blind or visually impaired person will *always* need help. Some are very independent and resent attitudes that may appear to be patronizing.

☐ Don't raise your voice when speaking to a person with a vision loss. They are visually impaired, not deaf, and they can hear you just fine.

☐ Don't ask their companions about them as if they were not there. If you want to know whether they have a need, ask them directly.

☐ Don't leave doors half opened and chairs pulled out. They can create a real obstacle course for those who are blind or visually impaired.

☐ Don't nod your head to indicate "yes" or "no." The blind and visually impaired often can't tell which direction your head is moving.

☐ Don't be afraid to offer orientation when a meal is served. Place the meat directly in front of the visually-impaired person and identify the location of other foods on the plate as well as the location of the beverage and utensils.

☐ Don't exclude them from regular church activities like men's or women's fellowships, mission trips, Acquire, music ministry, visitation outreaches, usher teams, Sunday School classes, and Bible studies. People who are blind, visually-impaired, or have some other physical disability, may need transportation, a little extra orientation, or other minor special considerations in order to participate, but they can offer a lot in return. The local church has an obligation to them to help them find their place in ministry so they can fulfill their role in the body of Christ. (See 1 Corinthians 12.)

Methods for Making Sunday School Accessible for Blind Children

The following techniques will help Sunday School teachers include blind or visually-impaired students more effectively in their classrooms.

Hands-on Activities

Children learn best when they're able to personally participate in an activity. This is also true of blind children. "Learning by doing" is a very effective learning technique, and blind students should be encouraged to participate along with the entire class. When using Play-Dough, blocks, etc. in tactile learning activities, each student should be encouraged to get involved whether or not they have visual limitations. By making adaptations where necessary, this playing field can be kept even. Blind children are far more capable than many people think. By demonstrating a positive attitude, the teacher can lead the entire class by example.

Here are some practical ways of using hands-on activities with children who are blind or visually impaired.

- ☐ Emphasize interaction among the students. If other students appear to be shy around the blind student because he or she is "different," make an extra effort to show your students how to include their blind classmate in the different activities. Hands-on time is a good time to do this. Having students share a container of crayons or a certain color Play-dough etc. is a great way for your students to learn that blind children can play and share just like other children.

- ☐ Encourage them to use their hands and fingers in the learning process. Encourage them to write, draw, use manipulatives which are objects designed to be moved or arranged by hand in order to develop motor skills or understand abstract ideas, musical instruments, etc. and involve the emotions and feelings while learning.

- ☐ Increase tactile clues by adding color, increasing the size, or moving objects closer. For example, when playing with a ball, use bright, air-filled, large, lightweight, plastic beach balls, Nerf balls, balloons, or the new, large soft, lightweight volleyballs.

- ☐ Pair children in physical activities so they work in partnership. Walking, jogging slowly, hopping for 60 seconds on first one and then two feet, etc. while holding hands can encourage children with visual limitations to become more active.

Kinesthetic Learning

Every teacher should learn to recognize and accommodate the learning styles of their students. Four learning styles are generally recognized: visual learning (through sight), auditory learning (through hearing), tactile learning (through touching), and kinesthetic learning (through motion). Although it is commonly assumed that all blind people are very strong auditory and/or tactile learners, this is not always the case. Many blind children are kinesthetic learners. Therefore, it is vital that the Sunday school teacher knows how to structure the lesson so that each student can maximize their learning potential.

Kinesthetic students learn more effectively when their bodies are in motion. They take in information best through the movement of their large or gross motor muscles. In any given classroom, you will see several children fidgeting with toys, shoes, hair, their neighbor, etc. during times that are designed to be focused on learning. Even though kinesthetic learning is one of the four major learning styles, often little emphasis is given to developing this learning style in a positive manner. Many teachers only see these children as "distracted," and they don't know how to turn the need to stay in motion to their advantage in the classroom.

- Kinesthetic learners retain more information when they are handling something. Divert a student who is picking on his neighbor by giving him a stress ball, Koosh ball, or lump of modeling clay, etc. to hold while learning. These tools can be very effective as long as the children understand that these objects cannot be thrown or tossed during the learning time.

- If the student feels self-conscious, the stress toy doesn't need to be apparent to the whole class. The student can use it in his or her lap without anyone seeing it. In his way, the student can take advantage of his specific learning style and gain great things from the class time without being a distraction or hindrance to others.

- Kinesthetic children learn while doing so have them "act out" songs, Bible stories, or segments of the lesson. Provide activities which allow them to learn while standing up or using their large arm muscles to write on a flip chart or chalk board. Get them involved in the discovery process, role-playing, simulations, building something that illustrates an element of the lesson, etc. Involve them in real-life activities. Use them as helpers so that they can use their bodies and movement in beneficial ways in the classroom.

Coloring and Craft Time

When students are coloring or engaged in other crafts, blind students can be involved if a few simple adaptations are made. Using tactile objects such as yarn, textured cloth, and stencils will help them get involved. If the class is coloring a picture of a snowman, buttons, bobbins, or other round objects might be used for the eyes, nose, mouth, and buttons on the snowman's belly. The outline of the snowman could be accentuated by gluing yarn onto the outline. This way, blind or visually impaired students will be able to feel the outline even though they may not be able to see it very well. Since blind students cannot pick up details visually, it is very helpful if they can learn through their sense of touch. The list of items that might be used in the classroom is limited only by the imagination of the Sunday School teacher or assistant. Some useful items include:

- ☐ Cotton balls (for clouds etc.)
- ☐ Sandpaper used to emphasize a certain object or area
- ☐ Textured fabrics to illustrate the clothing of a character
- ☐ "Puff" paint to outline objects or spell out words

Parents

Every Sunday School teacher knows that parental contact is vitally important. It is especially important to develop contact with the parents of students who are blind, visually impaired, or have other disabilities. Parents can help a teacher better understand a child's individual learning style and discover how to motivate and help that child succeed. Family members are the ones who spend the most time with a child. They have years of experience observing things that the teacher may not see, and they are aware of needs the teacher may not recognize. Cooperation between parents and teachers is not only helpful, it is vital. It can also be an incredible witness though which unsaved parents can find the Lord Jesus Christ. If you show parents that you care enough about their child who is living with a disability to go the extra mile to help them, it is an awesome testimony and a positive reflection of Christ.

Affirmation

Notice the areas in which individual students excel, and then encourage them to develop their strengths and areas of giftedness. Give them the support they need to flourish and pursue the areas of interest about which they are passionate or show particular talent. Affirmation is important to every student, but it can make a world of difference to a child who is blind or has some other physical or mental disability. Because the blind student may be self-conscious about his or her disability, affirmation is a central. Some have been teased by classmates. Sometimes they've been told by adults that they "won't amount to much." Sadly, many internalize this negative input and begin telling themselves that they "can't do anything." Nothing can be further from the truth. God has created each of us with unique talents and abilities, and He desires to use those gifts for His purposes. Affirmation can be the life-changing factor in a child's perception of his or her self-image.

Affirmation has the power to change an attitude that says, "I can't ever do anything right" to "I can do anything through Christ who gives me strength!" If a teacher affirms their God-given strengths and gifts, students can accomplish great things as they explore new avenues of learning and develop their abilities.

Relationship with Christ

Anyone can have a dedicated, dynamic, and life-shaping relationship with Christ - even someone with a disability. Feelings of discouragement and low self-esteem can make a blind child think he or she is "not good enough" for Jesus. It is important to be aware of this, and help each student to understand the truth of the gospel. Jesus died for them, and He loves them and wants a relationship with them. Remember, you, the teacher, are the role model that reflects Jesus. Children learn far more from example than they do from what you tell them. Give Christ to a child, and he will grow to give Christ to the world.

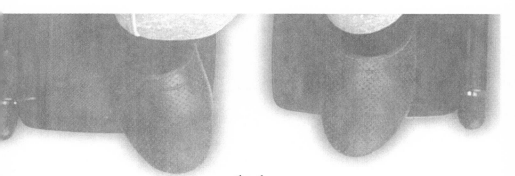

11.

A Shepherd for All of the Sheep: Pastoral Care and People Impacted by Disability

OBJECTIVES

- ☐ Understand the destructive nature of the fear of disability.
- ☐ Understand the five aspects of pastoral care and how they relate to people impacted by disability.

THE CONCEPT

All people who are disenfranchised by society, including people with disabilities, are looking for a local Shepherd who will embrace them as creations and children of God and who will stand up and say in Jesus' name and on His behalf: "These are mine! They belong to me!"

Foundation Scripture

Matthew 9:36

INTRODUCTION

This chapter briefly looks at several concepts discussed throughout this book from the standpoint of the local pastor. This chapter is deliberately brief because people with disabilities essentially require the same things from a pastor that every other member of the body needs: love, guidance, the ministry of the Word etc. However this chapter may help the local pastor see his ministry from a slightly different perspective.

Even if a church has the best outreach to people with disabilities in the local community that it could possibly have, and even if the church has a compassionate, caring and involved congregation and a staff that is energetic and sensitive to the needs of people with disabilities *there is still a unique role that only a Senior Pastor as shepherd of that congregation can fill. This role cannot be delegated and must not be abdicated.*

The unique role of the pastor involves setting the agenda for evangelizing people with disabilities in the first place and making it a life-and-death priority for the ministry of that local church. Remember it was the shepherd himself who left the ninety and nine and went after the lost sheep. That duty was not delegated and it was not abdicated. *A pastor does not have to wait for God to stir the heart of someone in the congregation to bring Christ to people with disabilities because his own heart should already be burdened.* It is also the pastor who will set the tone for the congregation by his example of personal interaction as to how people with disabilities will be received into the church family. *No one will open their arms wider or more enthusiastically than the Pastor.*

No matter what else is being done in a church to reach people with disabilities the Senior Pastor has a unique role to fill because he is the one who sets the agenda of outreach priorities and sets the tone by his example for how people of all kinds are received into the church family.

THE DESTRUCTIVE NATURE OF THE FEAR OF PHYSICAL AND MENTAL DISABILITY

It is not uncommon for anyone to have some kind of negative reaction the first-time they are exposed to physical and/or mental disability. Disability can be very intimidating and uncomfortable. Sometimes a fearful reaction is not only understandable it can be seen as natural. Human beings are naturally fearful of what they don't understand or are unfamiliar with. That being said, any Christian, but especially a pastor or church leader, by virtue of their call, does not have the luxury to respond negatively or fearfully to people with disabilities. Using an actual example, let's examine what can happen if leaders do not illuminate or control their fear or anxiety regarding disability.

Alexander is a gifted and anointed singer and Bible teacher. Many who have listened to him and are in a position to make such a judgment consider him to be one of the best Bible teachers in the United States. He was also an associate pastor and part of a large church staff in the western part of the country. While the senior pastor appreciated the giftedness of his protégé and staff member he was unable to embrace the fact that Alexander is also a quadriplegic. In the several years that Alexander served on his staff, the senior pastor never had a one-on-one meeting with him or sent notes expressing encouragement or appreciation for his service. There was one instance where a meeting was scheduled for several weeks and then canceled at the very last minute.

Actually the senior pastor may have had great guilt or anguish over his inability to confront his feelings. He was not only creating a difficult situation on his staff by modeling an uncomfortable relationship with an associate with a disability, he was also unknowingly fostering an atmosphere of alienation that would carry over into the church at large. Second Timothy 1:7 is a reminder from the apostle Paul that Christians cannot allow themselves to be intimidated by people or situations because we are on a mission of redemption and we are infused, empowered, motivated and controlled by the love of God which governs our thoughts, words, attitudes and reactions. Pastors and church leaders can overcome their personal fears and anxieties by keeping a daily journal, having routine fellowship with an accountability brother or talking about their feelings with a very close friend or fellow leader.

THE FIVE ASPECTS OF PASTORAL CARE

There are five elements that people who are disenfranchised are looking for in the pastor of their local church. These five elements can be examined by looking at the word **PASTOR** as an acronym.

Protection

People with disabilities and others who are disenfranchised are looking for a local church that will be a refuge of protection from the insensitivity, harassment and downright danger they face daily living in a world that is growing increasingly more intolerant of those with weaknesses, infirmities and limitations. They are looking for pastors who will help them deal with the personal pain their disabilities and other problems create in their life. They need help learning how to protect and insulate themselves from the anger and ignorance they confront daily with the love of Jesus Christ. In some sense they need their pastor to be a source of support who will stand by them and also be a champion, who when needed, will stand up for them against all forms of abuse.

Acceptance

After a while people with disabilities learn that they experience different levels of acceptance from the world around them. The levels of acceptance from the most minimal to the most complete are as follows:

1. Obligation out of Pity: "I will interact with you because I feel sorry for you."

2. Obligation out of Relationship: "I will interact with you because we are family."

3. Obligation out of Duty or Service: "I will interact with you because it's my job or my calling."

4. Adulation or Hero Worship: "I will interact with you because I think your disability is cool."

5. Respect: "I will interact with you because I admire or respect the way you face adversity."

6. Friendship: "I like you, disability or no disability."

7. Invisibility: "Disability? What disability?"

These levels are fairly self-explanatory and actually follow a biblical pattern from 1 Samuel 16:7: *"Man looks at the outward appearance, but the LORD looks at the heart."* The common experience of many people with disabilities is that when people first meet them all they see is a physical or mental impairment or maybe a piece of equipment or some kind of perceived deformity. After a period of time acceptance grows deeper and more complete until the disability becomes invisible. The disability, its realities and its demands, are still there but they no longer act as a barrier to friendship, warmth, love, interaction and appreciation.

In an ideal world of ideal Christians, Christians should not have to work through the different levels of acceptance in their relationships with people with disabilities. There is a much faster shortcut. The shortcut is to recognize the transforming power of the love of Jesus Christ that already resides in us (Romans 5:5) and to surrender to that transformation and allow it to manifest itself in all of our relationships. The life experience of many Christians is that they do work through the levels of acceptance to a certain extent but the dynamics of their Christianity (the love of God, the Word of God, prayer, and the Holy Spirit within them) greatly accelerate the acceptance process.

Accepting and appreciating people with disabilities simply as people that God has created and loves still requires that we deal with the reality and necessities of those disabilities. We can love them as individuals with every fiber in our being but they still have "feet to wash": urinals to empty, wheelchairs to push, language boards to deal with, etc.

One Senior Pastor in Wisconsin didn't just have people with disabilities in his congregation he also had them on his staff. He had to learn to tolerate and accommodate their disabilities in unique ways. The pastor did not find this to be difficult or grievous because he appreciated the giftedness and anointing of both young men. But occasionally it could be an almighty challenge. During a morning worship service an associate pastor, who was also quadriplegic who had developed narcolepsy fell asleep right at the point where the pastor was bringing his message to a dramatic conclusion. Right as he was about to make the ultimate point of the morning message the associate pastor fell out of his wheelchair. The following week his other young associate, who had no apparent disabilities, suddenly fell out of his pew with epilepsy at the same point of the service.

You can imagine how humiliated and mortified these two young ministers and their families were. They both revered their pastor as a mentor and were terribly embarrassed. But because he loved both of them as sons he was able to put the interruptions to his messages aside. The point is that pastors who integrate people with disabilities into their worship services need to be prepared for disruptions of many kinds and to respond to them with the acceptance, humor and grace of Christ.

A Parent's Perspective

Peter and Beverly Scheuermann, parents and foster parents to scores of special-needs children offer the following personal perspective on the acceptance a family impacted by physical and intellectual disability needs from a pastor and a church.

Hiding people with disabilities should have ended when the story of David's love for Jonathan's son Mephibosheth was told. However it seems that many people want to live in a world that is free from the problems that those with disabilities live with everyday. Our experience has been caring for and trying to meet the needs of those who are both mentally and physically challenged. Their comprehension is sometimes very limited.

Their number one need is to be accepted. They themselves love unconditionally. If only we who live without physical or mental challenges could love unconditionally as they do, what a wonderful world this would be.

Just in the last ten years we have been so pleased to see that building codes have included ramps into our churches and public buildings and accessible bathrooms in public places. Some churches have also made progress in making their aisles wide enough for wheelchairs to pass freely. Some churches even clear their front row so that people with disabilities can sit up front. Yet other churches still fail to realize that these simple accommodations for people with special-needs demonstrate acceptance or a lack of it.

When congregations experience first-hand exposure to people with disabilities and the needs they face, they have a serious personal choice to make in their own heart: How will they respond to what they have seen and experienced? Will they simply accommodate them out of pity, which can be done at a distance with no great personal investment, or will they return the unconditional love and acceptance that people with disabilities and special-needs have given to them?

Solace

The local pastor is a spiritual authority figure and that position impacts greatly on the solace or comfort and encouragement he provides to the people with disabilities that he consoles, counsels and interacts with. People with disabilities often need a tremendous amount of comfort and reassurance regarding their position in the Kingdom of God. They have questions such as: "Now that I'm 'broken' does God still have a plan for my life? Can God still use me in ministry? Will someone still want to marry me someday?" A pastor may have to answer these questions in many ways from the same individual many, many times as the person with the disability examines their life from different angles.

The calm, steady, reassuring, authoritative voice of a man or woman of God during a crisis period in the life of a person with a disability can make a tremendous difference in whether that individual goes on or gives up. It can be of great encouragement to simply remind them that no tragedy in their life takes God by surprise, and God gives them breath because He has a purpose in mind for them.

Time

People with disabilities daily encounter a lot of folks who for one reason or another have no time for them. This is especially true for those who have intellectual disabilities. When someone in authority such as a pastor chooses to spend time with people with disabilities, either individually or corporately, it helps them to feel validated. It helps them feel that they are worth the air they breathe and the space they occupy on the planet. Investing time in people with disabilities goes a tremendously long way in communicating God's love to them in a real way. They see that if a pastor thinks they are worthwhile and valuable it is not hard to believe that God thinks they are worthwhile and valuable.

It is hard to overestimate the role that a pastor plays in the validation process of a person with any kind of disability. *They often view their pastor as a spiritual leader, a father figure, and a protector. In other words, Pastor, many people with disabilities, whether they be physical or intellectual, look to you as a combination of Billy Graham, Ward Cleaver, Batman, and Jesus Christ Himself. They don't just see you as "Pastor so and so from First Church" they see you as their personal spiritual champion. To them you are "Super Pastor!"* Enormous weight is placed on your words, opinions and actions. Your validation through spending time with them, encouraging them, loving them, joking with them, touching their lives personally as well as from the pulpit will be one of the most lasting and meaningful things that you ever do in your ministry. By the same token, non-verbal messages of neglect, indifference and disinterest through non-participation in their lives may be devastating.

Dr. Howard Young, pastor of a major church in the Milwaukee area had only recently been installed when he visited a Special Touch Chapter Meeting that was taking place in the church on a Saturday afternoon. The group was made up of about thirty people with intellectual disabilities, ten people with physical disabilities and several parents and other people. Pastor Young observed the service and then during the fellowship time went around to each table and spoke to every single person and welcomed them to the church and spoke to them at some length. He didn't identify himself as the pastor. He simply went to each one, shook their hand and said, "I'm Howard, we're so glad to have you today." At first the people in the group looked at one another and said, "Who is that guy anyway?" Slowly it went around the room that the man who was spending so much time with them was the pastor of the church. They were so impressed and appreciative that he would take time to spend with them. The Special Touch Chapter had been meeting there for many years but this was the first time a pastor had participated.

Often pastors find that there are people in a congregation, who may or may not have disabilities that will become addicted to a pastor's time and attention. Sometimes this can become an issue with people with intellectual disabilities. But this is an occupational hazard and can be overcome through thoughtfulness and prayer.

Ordinances

In some churches a pastor may have to deal with members of the congregation who are not comfortable with people with disabilities, especially those with intellectual disabilities, receiving the ordinances of the church. Just like children, the vast majority of people with intellectual disabilities can receive the ordinances of the church with proper instruction. A pastor needs to take a Biblical stand on the issue and teach that standard to the congregation.

As people with disabilities begin to take their places in church leadership certain modifications may have to be made in the way the ordinances are conducted. In most every case appropriate accommodations can be made for whatever complications disability may present and still maintain the dignity and solemnity of the ordinances.

Respect for God's Gift and Call

Almost every person with a disability who is involved in one way or another in some form of ministry, either as a lay person in a local church or as a credentialed minister, in one denomination or another, does so because at one time or another a pastor, minister or other spiritual leader had respect for the call of God in their life and expressed confidence in their ministry gifts.

Charlie Chivers, Executive Director of Special Touch Ministry, Inc. has helped encourage scores of people with disabilities to explore their giftedness, answer God's call and venture out in faith. Within his own organization he mentors those with a call to ministry and provides opportunities that reflect where that individual is in developing their ministry. His respect for God's gift and call to people with disabilities has resulted in local churches that have been dynamically changed, men and women that have gone on to making an impact in various types of ministry across the country as pastors, evangelists, Christian educators, singers and musicians. His philosophy of providing personal encouragement and practical opportunity has also helped birth ministries of national importance. Any pastor who adopts this same kind of philosophy will have a profound impact on the Kingdom of God simply by sowing seeds of encouragement and opportunity.

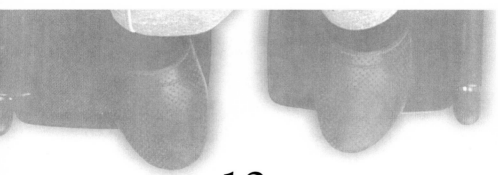

12.

The Forgotten Victims: Providing Encouragement and Respite to Caregivers

OBJECTIVES

- ☐ To understand the "dry well dilemma."

- ☐ To understand how caregiving changes relationships.

- ☐ To understand the multiple dimensions of weariness.

- ☐ To understand why caregivers may initially be resistant or reluctant to taking respite.

- ☐ To learn the necessary components of a quality respite program.

THE CONCEPT

An essential part of ministering to people with disabilities is ministering to their caregiver. The local church needs to develop ways to "lift up the hands that hang down."

Foundation Scripture

Exodus 17:11-13

INTRODUCTION

This chapter continues the discussion of caregiving that began in Chapter 9. For the most part we will continue to address the issue within the context of marriage. However most of the material will apply to most caregiving situations no matter what the relationship is between the caregiver and the person with the disability.

The phrase "the forgotten victims" was originally coined to describe family caregivers of Alzheimer's patients. It is equally appropriate to apply it to anyone who cares for a loved one on a long-term basis who will never get better.

The Purpose of Respite Ministry

The purpose of respite ministry is to recognize that many families impacted by physical or intellectual disability are not able to cope by themselves with the additional work, responsibility and stress that disability brings with it into family life. The local church then seeks to provide rest, relief and practical help so that family members do not break down and wear out physically, mentally emotionally or spiritually.

A key component of respite care is giving the primary care provider essential time and space away from the care environment.

Types of Respite Help

The frequency of respite help needed and the type of help required varies tremendously from family to family. Every situation is unique to itself. Some may require one hour every day or two hours three times a week. Others may only require one or two days a month while still others may need an entire week every six months. Most situations end up being some combination of the above.

Typical kinds of respite help needed include but are not limited to the following:

- ☐ Personal care provider or personal care assistance for a person with a physical disability

- ☐ Companion care for an elderly person or a person with a physical or intellectual disability so that the primary caregiver may get out for a few hours to attend to other responsibilities or to simply take a break

- ☐ Help with housekeeping

- ☐ Help with yard work and routine home maintenance and snow removal

- ☐ Provide care during primary caregiver breaks and vacations

The services in the list above are those routinely provided by County respite services. The list is not unreasonable, unrealistic or excessive. (Although many counties provide for the respite and support services listed above, most families impacted by disability do not receive them either because they do not meet the financial qualifications or they are stuck somewhere on a waiting list.)

Qualifications for Respite Workers

Believe it or not, most of the help required by primary caregivers is unskilled help to do the ordinary, everyday things everyone does. Even learning procedures for providing personal care to people with physical disabilities is not difficult. It does require someone who is a good listener, who can remember and follow the instructions they are given precisely. They must also be willing to ask questions when they don't understand a procedure or the reason behind it; and to keep asking until they get an answer they are satisfied with.

The ideal respite care worker is warm: friendly and engaging without being overpowering. They are pleasant, easy-going and present themselves well. They are in good physical condition. They are reliable, teachable and trustworthy. They are careful and thorough in their work and they clean up behind themselves. It is common for respite workers and families they serve to develop a warm, close personal relationship. The respite worker often becomes a part of an extended family.

What the Respite Worker and the Families They Serve Have the Right to Expect from One Another

☐ The relationship between a respite ministry worker and the family they are working with is based on mutual respect, trust and cooperation.

☐ Both parties need to respect the time of the other and keep scheduled appointments and notify the other if there are any changes.

☐ *Families always have to remember that the respite ministry worker is not an employee but a Christian friend ministering as unto Jesus Christ and should be treated accordingly and never taken for granted.*

☐ The two parties may be working together in the early and/or late hours of the day and need to have mutual tolerance for early morning/late night idiosyncrasies.

☐ The privacy and confidentiality of the relationship needs to be respected at all times by all parties. What is said, or what happens in the home stays in the home. (With the proviso that excludes issues of abuse or other issues that require a mandatory report to authorities.)

Truisms about Caregiving

Here are some common sentiments expressed by caregivers:

"What wears me down is that no matter how well I plan my day, no matter how good I am at what I do, my best is never good enough."

"In caregiving there is no such thing as being done."

"Her needs always exceed my resources."

"I know we're in trouble when his total incapacity meets my total exhaustion."

"It's not respite if I have to redo everything when I get back because care procedures were not done correctly by the respite worker and a medical problem now exists where none existed before. Who says I'm not indispensable?"

"If they [the respite care worker] would do the procedures exactly as I explained how they must be done, they would not find me so intimidating. I'm not intimidating. I'm just tired of cleaning up their messes and mistakes."

WARNING! The following comments may be offensive to some readers.

Here is a reflection of one Christian wife after caregiving for her quadriplegic husband for nineteen years:

In the last 19 years- - -
I sat in ICU from June 27 to July 14.
I fed him ice chips.
I cried while he slept.
I did this 10-12 hours a day, 7 days a week.
I was there when they took the screws out of his head.
I rode in the extra seat on the transfer plane and then in the ambulance that took him to rehab.
I do bowel programs and clean up puke.
I have taken care of blisters on his feet, a sore on his hip, and a variety of "places" on his tushy.
I nursed pneumonia once.
I take urine specimens by straight cath.
Between Memorial Day and August 15 this year, he had heat exhaustion three times. I took care of that.
Also since Memorial Day, I have cleaned up blood and learned to use gauze and tape as well as most of nurses I have encountered. The nurse told me so.
I have cleaned up diarrhea so bad that it flowed from the end of his pants leg.

More than once I had to "power wash" it out of the cave of his wound. The stuff was like water and it filled the wound and since you don't want that kind of infection going on so you clean it.
He was so sick anyway-2 or 3 infections from other things anyway. The fevers in Sept. and Oct.-one that spiked out at 103.9.
Got him to the doctor, took care of him…and managed to present a relatively healthy patient to the surgeon in Madison by Nov. 10.

You learn emergency first aid in school. You're supposed to call someone first. There was no one to call. None of our neighbors were even home. There was hardly time to think-only time to act and pray that it was the right thing to do.

Nobody asked me to do it. Some don't understand why I did it then or why I do what I do now. Some don't think I have any idea what I'm doing.
What am I supposed to do when he's blazing hot, talking crazy nuts from that fever, or blowing gallons of fluid from one end or the other? Or doing all of this all at once? What if I had waited or been sickened by the whole thing? Would he be here?

Nobody asked me to do this.
I didn't dream about doing this when I was a young girl.
I don't do it because I'm noble.
I don't even do it because I think I can do this any better than anyone else.
I don't do it because it's expected. I just do it.
And I'm ok with that.
(Written 2002)

The same couple is about to celebrate their 26th wedding anniversary. She is still his loving wife and caregiver. And she's still okay with it.

The "Dry Well" Dilemma

The life of a caregiver is a life of perpetual motion. It is a place where the idea of "running on empty" is all too often a day-to-day reality. A typical caregiver who provides for a spouse, a parent, a child or a sibling with a disability is usually on call 24/7/365. They are either on the go constantly providing some aspect of personal care for their "primary" or they are engaged in a life management activity such as cooking meals, doing laundry, paying bills, grocery shopping or any one of the myriad other chores that have to be done daily to keep a household of any size whatsoever together. The lifestyle of a caregiver is often way out of balance where work and serving the needs of other people is concerned. Rarely are they able to take time to be supported and nurtured themselves, pursue interests they enjoy or replenish their vitality and energy levels. *Without taking adequate time for rest, recreation and personal growth and renewal, the tasks of caregiving become burdens that ultimately grow too heavy to bear because they are trying to serve others from a "dry well."*

Over the course of time they lose touch with their personal goals and dreams. They can actually lose their sense of their own individuality and unique identity and begin to define themselves primarily or strictly as a caregiver.

"In caregiving there is no such thing as being done."

How Caregiving Changes Relationships

When a relative suddenly becomes a caregiver it can threaten and possibly change the dynamics of the relationship if the caregiver cannot maintain a Christ-like attitude and a servant's heart about what they are doing for the other person. As time passes, the danger to the relationship can increase if there is no respite. Here are four ways a relationship can change for the worse:

- ☐ The caregiver can begin to have the perception that they are doing all of the giving in the relationship and the other person is doing all of the receiving.

- ☐ The relationship can become adversarial and all of the joy and friendship can drain out of it because of the power struggle that can develop over who is in control of the care.

- ☐ Over the course of time the personal nursing care that is provided causes the relationship to become impersonal and clinical for some reason between a husband and a wife and the romantic sexual side of their relationship can evaporate.

□ Perspective is the ability to see both sides of the caregiving relationship. Loss of perspective on the part to the caregiver is a significantly dangerous first step that can lead to self-pity, anger and ultimately different types of abuse.

All marriage relationships and all personal relationships of any kind are threatened with erosion if both parties are not sensitive and aware of this possibility. The caregiver can do their part by not allowing the relationship to wear them down. They might take time to re-energize through respite and renewal and to try to maintain perspective.

The person in the relationship with the disability can respond by being appreciative of their caregiver, demonstrably cherishing them, and regularly and earnestly lifting them up before Jesus in intercession. Relationship maintenance has to be an ongoing priority. The second law of thermodynamics is that things always wind down. Therefore it's vital to always remember that passivity kills and destroys relationships and passion energizes them. But they do not maintain themselves. The passion has to be invested by the participants.

**Indifference and passivity kills and destroys relationships.
Passion and compassion energizes and restores them.**

The Multiple Dimensions of Weariness

The Physical Dimension

Improper Rest

By virtue of the definition of the job it is almost impossible for a "primary caregiver" to get enough rest. Their days are filled with non-stop work. It falls into three categories: caregiving chores, household and family chores, and economic support such as a part-time or even full-time job. If there are children to care for of any age whatsoever, another dimension is added to the problem. Many people who do not face the added wear and tear of caregiving are exhausted by their daily routine.

The nights are often as busy as the days. It is very difficult to get eight hours of solid sleep and good rest. Many people with disabilities have to be turned at least twice during the night. Some dehydrate easily and need periodic drinks of water. Often there are bouts with muscle spasms, indigestion, heartburn, occasional vomiting, autonomic dysreflexia with night sweats and blood pressure spikes, catheters and other plumbing that becomes disconnected, involuntary bowel movements and diarrhea. This is only a partial list. The possible disruptions are almost endless. It is a very rare thing for a caregiver to be able to start the day completely refreshed and revitalized.

Improper rest affects the caregiver in every other area of their life. It impacts their ability to provide care, their mood, their appetite, their general energy level, their perception of themselves and their relationships with others. If "improper rest" becomes a pattern or descends into sleep deprivation the behavior may become erratic and their perception of reality could be seriously affected. The bottom line is the improper rest cannot be treated lightly because it has a direct impact on the physical and mental health of both the caregiver and their primary.

Improper Technique

This one is not all that common because most caregivers are able to get some kind of professional training or coaching at the outset. Occasionally however, there will be someone who is thrown into the process of caregiving so quickly and that they don't have the time to learn the proper procedures, body mechanics and the dynamics of leverage and lifting that can save them years of pain, frustration and chiropractor bills.

Some caregivers resist learning proper techniques because they just don't like to ask for help or feel that asking for help reflects badly on them as a person. There is nothing wrong and certainly nothing shameful about learning a new way of doing bed rolls, dressing, lifts or transfers that will save you time, energy, frustration and years of pain and loss of flexibility in your back and joints.

Inadequate Equipment

Caregivers may also put themselves at risk physically if they do not have or do not use the equipment they need to do safe and proper transfers such as a transfer belt or Hoyer lift.

Repetitive Stress Injury

There is a part of caregiving that is very physical. The person under care needs to be rolled, lifted, dressed and transferred. They also need range of motion and other exercises. Over a period of time the caregiver develops their own individual way of doing these major physical activities into a way that is both comfortable and efficient. The downside of this personal physical shorthand they develop is that they end up doing the exact same tasks in the exact same way over a course of years. This means that the same muscles and joints are being stressed and strained in the same way, every day, with no relief. All of this regular wear and tear can produce repetitive stress injuries such as Carpal Tunnel Syndrome.

Here are a few things that caregivers can do to lower their susceptibility to RSI:

☐ Take a proactive approach to your health by understanding that your physical resources are limited and that your body will wear down over the course of time if you don't take care of it.

☐ Use the tips, tools and equipment that are available to make your life easier; don't make caregiving harder than it already is by thinking that you have to be an "Iron Man" or a "Wonder Woman."

☐ Listen to your body and don't ignore the signals that pain may be sending you; when you start feeling pain see your doctor.

The Advance of Age

The problems associated with growing older tend to sneak up on most caregivers. The one thing they slowly begin to notice is that they start to slow down a little. Doing care for their primary takes longer than it used to. Household management and everything else also takes longer. When a caregiver begins to sense that age is starting to sneak up on them they need to recognize that they will not be able to provide quality care forever. It is never too early to begin planning for respite and supplemental care, and ultimately permanent care solutions if you are unable to continue as the primary caregiver.

One area where the local church can help early on is to recognize the logistical nightmares that most families impacted by disability face on Sunday mornings. When a caregiver begins to slow down this may be an area where it shows up first. It is almost impossible to hire or get subsidized help for a Sunday morning. On top of that, the kind of help the caregiver needs would probably be fairly limited. The helper would not have to be a caregiving professional and would not have to do any complicated procedures. What the caregiver is looking for in this situation is simply an extra pair of hands to assist with bathing, dressing and ADL's (Activities of Daily Living, such as shaving, washing hair etc.) The caregiver needs this kind of help so that they can get themselves and any children ready for church.

This kind of "helping hands" ministry is the kind of thing any church should excel at and be able to implement easily. It does not have to become the burden of one person. It can easily be rotated from one individual to the other because the work required is unskilled. This is also the perfect type of entry-level caregiving for someone just starting out in ministry to people with disabilities because they can work up to the scarier areas of personal care gradually. Helping out on Sunday mornings is a simple yet powerful way to support caregivers and demonstrate in a practical way the love of Jesus Christ.

Other Physical Factors

Some other factors that affect the physical dimension of weariness for the caregiver concern their personal health regimen. Are they eating a nutritious diet? Are they keeping their weight down? Are they getting enough fresh air and exercise? Menopause, arthritis, osteoporosis and other conditions that may arise must also be considered.

The application here for the disability ministry worker underscores the main point of this entire chapter: A caregiver must have enough time in their personal life to successfully maintain their own physical, mental, the emotional and spiritual health. In order for them to have that time, the local church has to be able to step up and provide a respite program that is as comprehensive as possible.

The Mental and Emotional Dimensions

(Editor's Note: This chapter is not being written by mental health care professionals but by a couple who have had twenty-six years in a marriage and caregiving relationship with considerable ministry experience in pastoral care. The information offered in this section is based on day-to-day life experience as opposed to academic training and professional clinical experience. For additional information on this topic please consult a professional Christian counselor or mental health professional.)

The Stress of Imperfection

Caregivers not only live under the constant stress of wearing many different hats and having multiple responsibilities, they also live under the constant pressure to get it all right all of the time. It is no wonder then that a caregiver, who must juggle even more balls in the air at one time than the average person with a highly stressful life, will occasionally drop one.

One of the things that caregivers must occasionally contend with is a tendency on the part of the people who observe their day-to-day life to offer opinions and express judgmental attitudes regarding the quality of care they are providing rather than offering a kindly word of encouragement, an extra set of helping hands, or just a friendly cup of coffee. The emotional impact on caregivers living in this negative atmosphere can be illustrated using a sports analogy. For the caregiver, it is very much like running behind in a race that cannot possibly be won and suddenly having the crowd turn against you.

One of the problems with never being able to catch up with everything that needs to be done and occasionally "dropping one of the balls" that *must stay in the air* is that a certain amount of "slippage" occurs. Slippage is a snowballing effect where more balls get dropped and more and more things remain undone at the end of the day until there are stacks of dirty dishes and piles of dirty laundry is and the situation continues to become increasingly hopeless.

Anger

Sooner or later a caregiver will react emotionally to the relentless physical exhaustion and continuous stress. It may begin as expressions of self-pity such as, "This is so unfair!" or "I didn't ask for this!" Often a caregiver may express these feelings in more subtle and even nonverbal ways such as irritability, grudging cooperation, providing care without compassion or early signs of insensitive or neglectful care. Obviously these red flags are indicators of greater possible danger ahead if there is not immediate relief provided for the caregiver.

Guilt

Equally troubling and potentially dangerous is a situation where the caregiver turns the anger inward upon themselves by internalizing the negative attitudes of people in their life. Sometimes even the person they are providing care for can become a source of negativity and pain by being demanding and unappreciative. The caregiver who turns the anger inward does not see that the reality of the situation is that there is simply too much work in their life for one person to be able to consistently perform at a high rate of efficiency and get everything done, every day, without fail. Instead they believe that they are solely and completely to blame; that the problem lies in some failure in their character, skills or stamina. In reality, as well as in their mind and spirit they may hear the phrase, "Can't you do anything right?" several times a day. Eventually that statement becomes internalized and changes into the value judgment, *"I can't do anything right!"* Their anger turned inward becomes a form of guilt because they believe they have failed to provide loving and adequate care to their loved one.

Depression

Obviously people in the mental and emotional state described above need to seek immediate help. For caregivers that can be problematic for several reasons. First of all is the inability or refusal of the individual to recognize or to admit that they are in trouble. One anonymous caregiver said this: "Sometimes you don't realize you are in trouble until you find yourself hiding in the closet crying."

The ability to pay for diagnosis, treatment and counseling is another considerable hurdle that must be overcome. It's very easy for those in the orbit of the caregiver to recommend counseling and treatment but both can be prohibitively expensive for families impacted by disability living on a limited income. As of this writing the cost of weekly counseling sessions with a professional Christian counselor and medication can add over $600 to the family's monthly budget.

Fortunately there are some cost-effective choices for families facing this dilemma. Some Christian counseling services have sliding scale rates for families with lower incomes. Individual Christian counselors sometimes do pro bono work on the side for clients who cannot afford to pay. Many churches have pastors that do a considerable amount of pastoral counseling on many issues including depression. Some have professional counselors that they consult with. *Pastoral counseling has several limitations that the pastor and the counselee need to discuss in advance.*

A physician can also be of assistance in recommending cost-effective treatment measures. He may recommend herbal supplements rather than expensive prescription drugs. Sometimes he can provide samples of medication until an effective one can be found. *Each individual should discuss their entire treatment program with their physician, including their counseling and treatment options. No cost-effective alternatives should be explored without consulting with a family physician. It can sometimes be dangerous to take herbal supplements if you are or have been taking prescription drugs. All treatment for stress, depression or similar conditions should start with a visit to the family physician.*

Another reason that Christians can be resistant to getting help with depression is that in many churches and communities, mental and emotional distress or illness has an unfair stigma attached to it. People who need help are treated without compassion and labeled in a juvenile way by being called, "crazy," "Looney Tunes," or "wacko." A mental or emotional ailment is no different and is no less deserving of compassion than a physical or spiritual problem. Physical problems in the body often occur when things break down. Mental and emotional distress is often caused by the depletion or imbalance of certain chemicals or substances in the brain. *The role of the local church in the lives of people can never be overstated: it should be a source of the gospel message of redemption and also a "soft place to fall."*

"Sometimes you don't realize that you are in trouble until you find yourself hiding in the closet crying."

The Spiritual Dimension

The Bible makes it clear that life in this world is a continual spiritual battle against the forces of darkness (Ephesians 6:12). Life is spiritually draining on everyone, no matter what our circumstances are. A caregiver may have little time for anything more than devotional reading and attending Sunday morning service.

Caregivers are spiritually drained and very thirsty for Living Water, but there is one thing that can "taint the water." Sometimes people who are unable to attend church regularly or frequently are quite sensitive to that fact and worried that regular attendees and church members will be judgmental about their lack of regular attendance. If there is one thing that caregivers do not need from their church is another place where they feel that they have failed to measure up and meet expectations. *Church families need to treat burned-out caregivers the way a nurse would treat an ICU patient on life support; carefully, lovingly and tenderly.*

The Financial Dimension

According to the most recent census and Department of Labor statistics, a majority of families impacted by disability have an income of less than $15,000 per year. The constant worry over having enough to get by and to take care of unexpected medical emergencies and retire items like uninsured debt make it almost frivolous and inconceivable to plan for luxuries like a family vacation. As was stated in the companion chapter on marriage, the constant worry over finances drains a lot of the color and fun out of life because it's hard to be spontaneous without having at least a couple of extra dollars in your pocket.

Churches also need to be aware that this is also one reason why families impacted by disability do not participate more in church functions. So many church functions these days require at least a nominal cost. Many times a family dealing with disability, especially if they have several children, is not going to be financially able to afford even the nominal amount and they are often embarrassed if they have to ask about special consideration.

In these times when many families deal with frequent layoffs, job changes and financial shifts, churches need to re-examine their financial policies for programs and activities to make sure that they are financially and easily accessible to those disenfranchised groups who have always traditionally found refuge and relief in the church. Churches should also examine their policies and expectations concerning dress code to make sure that the church is socially accessible to those who may not be able to afford expensive wardrobes.

The Social Dimension

Gayle Leach, a schoolteacher, minister's wife, missionary and caregiver for her husband since 1983, made the following observations on the social dimension of weariness:

People outside the world of disability need to recognize that caregivers who have gone for long periods of time without respite cannot be expected to act normally in social situations because they are exhausted and they have experienced a certain amount of "shell shock." They have been at war, so to speak, and have been so worn out for so long that they have forgotten how much fun having fun can be to the point that it becomes so emotionally overwhelming.

The first time we came to a Special Touch Summer Get Away I had been caregiving for nearly three years without a break. I didn't really know I was supposed to take one. During that time we had started to deal with the aftermath of his car wreck, I started a new job, we got married, my parents separated and mom and sister came to live with us, my grandfather had died, my dad had major cancer surgery, Tom's sister committed suicide, his mother was paralyzed with French polio for a year and the list goes on and on. So by the time we got to the Get Away I was a mess. The sudden stress relief was almost too much to take all at once. I had been pressing down so much ugliness for so many months that it all suddenly came rushing out in a flood and I cried nonstop for four days.

The same type of thing happened the first time I attended a Special Touch retreat. Someone told a joke. I had not laughed in so long that I laughed until I cried and then I cried for twenty minutes and had to go back to my room. *This kind of behavior is not at all unusual for anyone who has gone for months and months without any fellowship, relaxation or social time whatsoever. Caregivers in that condition need to know that they have the freedom to decompress and recalibrate their emotional equilibrium.*

WHY CAREGIVERS MAY BE INITIALLY RELUCTANT TO TAKE RESPITE

- ☐ Pride: It's not easy to ask for or to accept help or admit that a job is just too big; the local church family needs to support and affirm caregivers by constantly reassuring them that asking for help is in no way an indication that they have failed.

- ☐ Guilt: Caregivers may feel a certain amount of misplaced guilt in taking time for themselves away from caring for their loved one, they may feel like they are abdicating their responsibility; again they need to be reassured that maintaining a healthy physical, mental, emotional, spiritual and social lifestyle is in the best interest of providing high-quality long-term care.

- ☐ Fear: Both the caregiver and their primary (the one they are caring for) are going to feel a little bit of fear in letting a respite care worker into their private world; the respite care worker has to understand going in that he or she is going to have to prove their worth and earned the trust they are being given, caregiving is a sacred trust and a confidential relationship of the highest order.

☐ They have to clean it up if you don't do it right: Mistakes are going to happen, they are part of the learning process, but leaving more work for the caregiver than they had when they left is counterproductive and destroys the whole purpose of having respite care in the first place.

☐ They may have to live with your serious mistakes for quite a while: Caregiving procedures are very precise and each person receiving care may do things a little bit differently. Individual variations must be respected and followed to the letter without creating shortcuts; if you are unable to do what is asked of you, find a new ministry. Taking shortcuts or leaving things undone creates serious complications that you will not have to pay the price for, you will not be the one confined to bed for weeks or months at a time, you will not have to pay the additional medical expenses.

Respite ministry workers and visitors from the church need to understand the fundamental truth of respite ministry: If everything in the home was functioning at 100% efficiency, there would be absolutely no need for respite ministry.

THE COMPONENTS OF A QUALITY RESPITE PROGRAM IN A LOCAL CHURCH

An Understanding Heart

As noted earlier, one of the reasons families impacted by disability are resistant to accept respite is because they are hesitant to allow a total stranger into their private world. They are afraid of being judged or of being labeled "dysfunctional." The essential truth that all respite ministry workers must remember is that they are working with families that live in a perpetual state of "crisis management mode," going from one crisis to the next. These families already know they have trouble, if they didn't they would have no need for your ministry. Be aware of the characteristics of the world you are entering into.

SOME CHARACTERISTICS OF THE WORLD OF DISABILITY

The Challenges of Time Management

Everything takes longer. As a result, to do everything that a person without a disability would do in the normal course of a day, a person with a disability and their caregiver must get up earlier and stay up later which contributes to their perpetual exhaustion. It is not uncommon for caregivers who also work full-time to have to begin their morning procedures by 4:30 a.m. in order to get their primary ready for the day and then get kids ready for school and be ready to roll out the door at 6:45 a.m. for their commute to work.

Reconciling the Demands of the Real World with the Realities of Life with a Disability

Joni Earickson Tada tells a story about going to take her written examination for her driver's test. First she was told that she would have to appear for the exam at eight o'clock in the morning. Joni and her caregiver considered it a red letter day if she was out the door by ten o'clock! Next, she was told that she would have to fill out a computerized answer sheet by filling in the little spaces with a number two lead pencil. Joni patiently explained to the clerk that she was a quadriplegic and no had use of her arms. The clerk then challenged her with the question, "If that's the case, why are you wasting your time taking your driver's test?" In this case, Joni not only had to contend with the unfair logistical demands of the test but also with the ignorance of the clerk.

Many people don't understand that it's not just a matter of multiplying the time it takes one person to get ready by two. There are extra components to the day of a person with physical disabilities that are part of the process of getting ready and there are some that just take longer. For instance, a morning bath or shower for a person without a disability may take ten or fifteen minutes. A person with a disability has to add time to their bath or shower just for getting in and out. Likewise a morning trip to the toilet which may normally take a maximum of fifteen minutes may take anywhere from fifteen minutes to three hours depending on the day.

Every activity of daily life from transportation, to meals, to getting ready to watch *Monday Night Football* will follow the same pattern of requiring more time in order to accommodate the disability.

The Drain to Maintain

People with disabilities expend a tremendous amount of energy just co-existing with their disability. Sitting for long periods of time, continual muscle spasms and dealing with chronic phantom pain creates physical, mental, emotional and spiritual fatigue and irritability which has an impact on their caregiver and on the family. Many people with physical disability look at it this way: It takes putting out a tremendous amount of energy just for them to get up to zero.

This is a very important dimension of life with disability that employers need to understand. Most people with physical disabilities are capable of being as productive as anyone else as far as output and work product is concerned. However they may require flexible conditions and a disability friendly working environment in order to reach that level.

Living Crisis to Crisis

Without the provision of regular respite, people with disabilities, their caregivers and families often live in a constant mode of crisis prevention. They are never able to step back and plan and prioritize how they are going to execute their responsibilities. Riding a constant whirlwind, always running behind and never able to approach the activities of daily living proactively creates a different perspective on what constitutes daily success.

An outsider may come into the home of a family impacted by disability at the end of the day and see different scenes of unfinished housework: dishes in the sink, a floor that needs to be vacuumed and a basket of laundry that needs to be put away. From their perspective today could have gone a little better and been more successful.

When the exhausted caregiver falls into bed that night, even as they acutely feel their shortcomings, they look back at the day from a different point of view. The day was a complete success. They can say to themselves: "Everybody got out of bed, everybody had clean clothes to wear, everybody got to school and to work more or less on time, there were no emergencies or accidents related to disability, everybody got home safely, everyone got fed and now I have five whole hours to sleep before I have to wake up and try to accomplish the same thing tomorrow."

Unpredictability

The following incidents actually happened to one person in a span of a little over two years: He is having dinner with his wife at a nice supper club when his wheelchair tire explodes causing a moment of terror in the restaurant because it sounded like a gunshot. He was going about his daily business downtown paying bills and running errands. Suddenly he was struck with violent diarrhea. This problem was complicated by the fact that he still had to take public transportation home. Later during the winter months, he and his wife came to church only to have the electric wheelchair lift and van doors malfunction. The lift would not stow properly so the doors could not close.

Everyone lives with an element of unpredictability in their lives but because of the multiplied medical and mechanical factors a person with a disability depends upon to cooperate moment by moment, there is a much higher probability that unpredictability will raise its ugly head and say, "Gotcha!" People who live in the orbit of people with disabilities don't always fully appreciate the impact the reality of unpredictability has on the decision-making process of a person with a disability. They often push too hard when they encourage a person with a disability to expand self-imposed boundaries.

For example if a man becomes a quadriplegic as a result of a car wreck and narrowly avoids killing a passenger, the people in his world need to respect his reservations and resistance to learning how to drive again. The individual living with the disability has learned to respect unpredictability. Although a Christian is commanded to live a life that is not dominated by fear, and the line between caution and fear can sometimes be very, very fine, the Christian with a disability must be allowed to make that call where his own life is concerned. Even if he never gets behind the wheel of another vehicle, he or she still deserves all due respect for having the courage for getting out of bed and going about his day with the knowledge that his power wheelchair may malfunction and fail in the middle of crossing a busy street or go berserk in the Electronics section of K Mart because of the electromagnetic interference caused by some kid trying out a video game. The person with the disability isn't having wild fantasies but has learned to face danger head-on through daily education in the school of disability.

Conclusion to Understanding Characteristics of the World of Disability

The bottom line that people from the local church and the members of a disability ministry team or respite care workers need to remember when entering the private world of a family impacted by disability is that each one of us is still a work in progress where Jesus Christ is concerned. Each of us still has imperfection in our thinking and behavior that we need to continue to work out in our walk through our day-to-day life as Christ orders our steps (Ps. 37:23). *In the meantime, Jesus understands our weaknesses and because He does understand them, our gaps and limitations do not disqualify us from His love or His service.* If Christ Himself is willing to be patient with our gaps and limitations, how much more should His body extend that same patience and grace to one another? (See Phil. 1:6; Psalm 138:8)

None of the characteristics above are excuses for failure by people with disabilities or their caregivers rather they are demonstrations that respite ministry is desperately needed.

Eyes that See

Caregivers are usually painfully aware of the areas of life where it may look to others like they are "dropping the ball." Not everyone outside the situation always sees the problem and interprets it correctly. People might drive by the home of a family impacted by physical disability and say, "Why don't they take better care of their lawn?" Or "Why don't they get their house painted?" They are mistaking the undone chores for apathy and shoddiness rather than a cry for help. "If they need help so bad, why don't they just ask for it?" The answers to this question are the same as those for why people resist taking respite care. In addition, many people with disabilities and their caregivers do call for help on certain friends and neighbors but are fearful of wearing out their welcome and abusing their hospitality and friendship.

Hands That Are Ready and Willing

One of the reasons people with disabilities and their caregivers do not say more when they need help is they have grown accustomed to people volunteering and then not following through. No one likes to sound like a nag. Being motivated by obligation or guilt helps no one. If you can't follow through on a promise to get a job finished in a timely manner let someone else know, or don't volunteer in the first place.

A Broad-based Network of Volunteers

The best way to approach ministry to people with disabilities as a mission of the local church and avoid burning out a few dedicated people is to have a vision that encompasses the ministry gifts and the callings of "every person in every pew."

Every person alive is either a missionary or a mission field.

The fundamental problem of some Disability Awareness Sunday programs is that 80 percent of the congregation has tuned out after the first five minutes. They watch the slides and are touched and repelled at the same time. Many of them make the snap decision that they aren't "special enough" for this kind of ministry. They make a rush to judgment and assume that they do not have in them what God is looking for to minister to these "special" people. They have a narrow view of what evangelizing people with disabilities is all about. We need more than just people who are willing to do personal care. We need people with *every conceivable kind of ministry gift. If a person is breathing and knows Jesus Christ, he or she has something they can contribute to the cause of evangelizing people with disabilities other than simply putting five dollars in the offering and taking a prayer card.*

Ministries to people with disabilities in the local church need every willing hand and willing heart from children who can fly kites, teenagers who can read aloud and do a little housework, men who can repair a flat tire or a broken screen or to women who like to drink coffee and have Bible studies, to the older women of the church who have a cookie ministry. *All of these and everyone in between can do something to touch the heart of a person with a disability, or a caregiver or a member of their family for Jesus Christ.*

When the local church follows the model of a healthy functioning body given in 1 Cor. 12 in the area of ministry to people with disabilities and their caregivers, as well as many other areas of church life, the labor of ministry is evenly distributed among the parts of the body and no one part fails, wears out or ceases to function.

When a church family joins hearts and hands together to reach into every segment of the community, every highway, every byway, every back alley, and shines the light of the gospel of Christ in every dark and shadowy place the disenfranchised will run into the wide open arms of those holding the light. Not every Christian can go to Africa, India or the Philippines but sometimes the most difficult missionary journey of all is to simply walk across the street, full of the love of Jesus, with a smile on your face and an apple pie in your hand, saying, "Hi, I'm your neighbor from across the street and I was just wondering if there is anything that I could do to help?"

Not everyone can go to Africa, India or the Philippines but sometimes the most difficult missionary journey of all is simply walking across the street to your neighbor's house in the name and love of Jesus Christ.

Afterword

In 1980 I was new in the ministry. I had been working as a tent making "missionary" with Child Evangelism Fellowship in Grand Forks, North Dakota. I lived right downtown, across the street from the Dakota Hotel.

One Sunday night in the late winter or early spring I got hungry and decided to walk to a nearby convenience store to pick up hot dogs and buns and a six pack of Coke. On the way through the darkened streets I was scared out of my wits by a German Shepherd dog left in the back of a pick up. After getting my groceries I decided to return home by a different route that took me past the city mission. Standing across from the mission was a short confused man with a suitcase without a handle and a large cardboard box. After I said, "Hi, I'm Tom," he explained his predicament.

His name was Albert and he had jut been thrown out of the mission for fighting. I knew the guy who ran the mission and knew there was no appeal for breaking the rules. Thus began the adventure of finding Albert a place to stay for the night. I had my grocery bag and he had the case so we stashed the unwieldy box under a tree. I promised I'd get it later and we set out. He didn't want the police and they didn't want him. I had no idea what to do so I called my CEF boss from the lobby of the Dakota because I didn't have a phone. This is where it started to get interesting.

He said, "Call the Salvation Army." And he gave me the number. I called and explained the problem and the SA officer replied, "Can you get him to the Dakota Hotel? We'll pay for one night and his breakfast."

Okay, I thought, God's in this somewhere. I got Albert registered and settled and went after the big box. When I returned with the box to Albert's room he was nowhere to be found. So now I'm roaming the deserted streets of downtown at 11:00 pm searching for Albert and calling his name. I finally find him. "Albert, what are you doing?"

"I'm looking for my box."

"It's in your hotel room."

"How did it get there?"

I was ready to spit nickels.

I got him resettled and said, "Albert, are you hungry?"

"Uh, yeah."

"Do you like hot dogs and Coke?"

"Uh, yeah."

I told him not to go anywhere and went across the street to fix his food. Thankfully when I brought it back he was still there. I said, "Okay Albert, you're all set. Good night," and I turned to leave. A familiar silent voice spoke to my heart and said, "You've seen to his physical needs. What about his spiritual needs?"

"But Lord, how? Albert can't understand."

"Albert is a grown child. Check your back pocket."

I always carried a small Wordless Book and a pocket New Testament and led Albert to Jesus. As much as this book is for those on the Dedication Page, it is also for Albert and all the Alberts I have left to encounter in my life and to lead them to Jesus.

God bless you Albert,
Tom Leach

About the Authors

Charlie Chivers is a nationally appointed missionary to people with disabilities as well as the president and founder of Special Touch Ministry, Inc. Since 1982, Special Touch has served the concerns of over 89,000 people in many states across the nation impacted by disabilities. Charlie speaks throughout the country at churches, conferences, camps and many other venues and functions on the topics of disability awareness, advocacy and evangelism. His passion is reaching this neglected mission field. He and his wife and ministry co-founder Debbie also coordinate the Wisconsin Special Touch Summer Get Away. The Chivers and Special Touch are based in Waupaca, Wisconsin.

Larry Campbell is a nationally appointed missionary to people with disabilities and has nearly thirty years of front line experience in evangelizing people with intellectual disabilities. He is recognized as one of the leading authorities in this specialized brand of ministry. Larry and his wife Carolyn travel across the country most of the year on a busy ministry schedule. Their passion is to establish a Special Touch Disability Ministry Training Center. They are based in Waupaca, Wisconsin,

Paul Weingartner, legally blind himself, is the Executive Director of the Assemblies of God Center for the Blind. With his wife Caryl, he travels each year speaking on issues relevant to the community of the blind. The mission of the Center is to produce and provide quality Christian materials of many types and kinds so that the blind and vision impaired and their families may fully participate in the life of the Church. That mission is Paul's passion. Paul and Caryl live in Springfield, Missouri.

Sarah Sykes is a trusted associate at the AG Center for the Blind and a certified Braille transcriber. She also has been involved in helping the blind and visually impaired participate in Christian Education programs in the local church.

Tom Leach has had a lifetime of experience with physical disability. He was born with very mild Cerebral Palsy and at age 25 was paralyzed from the chest down as a C 6-7 quadriplegic.

Tom and his wife Gayle experienced the dynamic way God uses Special Touch Ministry in 1986, when they began attending Summer Get Away. God used Special Touch to heal hurts caused by living with quadriplegia and to pave their way back into full-time ministry after Tom's car wreck in 1983. The couple has served on the ministry's full-time staff since 1995. They have worked intensively with people with mild intellectual disabilities since 1991. They now spearhead the development of new programs and products, such as the Word Walk Curriculum. Tom is also a novelist. Tom and Gayle represent Special Touch in the Dakotas and minister around the nation wherever God opens doors of opportunity. They currently live in Ellendale, North Dakota. Their passion is opening the doors of churches in America to people with disabilities.

Appendices

Appendix I
Ten Tips for Effective Communication with People who have Disabilities

DISABILITY ETIQUETTE:

1. When talking with a person with a disability, speak directly to that person rather than through a companion or sign language interpreter who may be present.

2. When introduced to a person with a disability, it is appropriate to offer to shake hands. People with limited hand use or who wear an artificial limb can usually shake hands, (Shaking hands with the left hand is an acceptable greeting.)

3. When meeting a person with a visual impairment, always identify yourself and others who may be with you. When conversing in a group, remember to identify the person to whom you are speaking.

4. If you offer assistance, wait until the offer is accepted. Then listen to or ask for instructions.

5. Treat adults as adults. Address people who have disabilities by their first names only when extending the same familiarity to all others present. (Never patronize people who use wheelchairs by patting them on the head or shoulder.)

6. Leaning or hanging on a person's wheelchair is similar to leaning or hanging on a person and is generally considered annoying. The chair is part of the personal body space of the person who uses it. However, this changes as people become friends.

7. Listen attentively when you're talking with a person who has difficulty speaking. Be patient and wait for the person to finish, rather than correcting or speaking for that person. If necessary, ask short questions that require short answers,

a nod or shake of the head. Never pretend to understand if you are having difficulty doing so. Instead, repeat what you have understood and allow the person to respond. The response will clue you in and guide your understanding.

8. When speaking with a person in a wheelchair or a person who uses crutches, if possible, place yourself at eye level in front of the person to facilitate the conversation.

9. To get the attention of a person who is hearing-impaired, tap the person on the shoulder or wave your hand. Look directly at the person and speak clearly, slowly and expressively to establish if the person can read your lips. Not all people with a hearing impairment can lip-read. For those who do lip-read, be sensitive to their needs by placing yourself facing the light source and keeping hands, cups, and food away from your mouth when speaking.

10. Relax. Don't be embarrassed if you happen to use accepted, common expressions such as "See you later, "or "Did you hear about this," that seem to relate to the person's disability.

Appendix II
Disability Ministry Registration Form

SAMPLE FORMS

Today's Date_____

Student's Name_____

Address_____

City_____ST_____Zip_____

Birthdate_____Phone_____

Parent's Names_____

Parent's Address_____

City_____ST_____Zip_____

Phone_____Cell_____

Brother(s)/Sister(s)- - -first names and ages_____

_____

School_____

Specific Type of Disability_____

Equipment needed_____

Communication Skills_____

Medications_____

Allergies: Food _____Pollen_____

Pet _____ Drinks _____

Other _____

Seizures _____

Any special fears? Specific behaviors _____

Is help needed for personal hygiene? _____

Medical issues that may require an aid or nurse _____

_____

Student's understanding of God and a relationship with Him _____

_____

Can student be released when class is over or should he/she stay and wait for an adult to pick him/her up? If so, please list the name and relationship of the person picking up your student. _____

Please add any information to the bottom and back of this sheet that will enable us to ensure that your loved one is comfortable and enjoys participating in our program.

Individual Spiritual Mentorship Plan

Student Name _____ D.O.B._____

Date of Mtg. To Develop/Review ISMP_____

Student's Address_____

City_____ST_____Zip_____

Phone_____

Student's Disability_____

Effects of Disability_____

How he/she can benefit from our program_____

_____

How does the student's disability affect their involvement and progress in a classroom setting? _____

_____

How does the student's disability affect their level of activity and participation with a group? _____

_____

Support Team Members (list needs to include, but is not limited to, the names of parents, disability pastor, youth/children's pastor, Sunday school teacher, small group leader/teacher, and head pastor)_____

"Buddy" (a volunteer-can be a peer- who stays with the student for the entire session)

_____

Start Date:

Specific Plan Form

Today's Date_____

Student's Name _____ Age _____

Student's address_____

City _____ST _____ Zip _____

Phone_____

Student's Disability_____

Class Placement_____

Support Team Members_____

_____

Start Date_____

Person Responsible/ Date Due: Specific Plan:
(Who takes care of what and when AND exactly how it is to be done)

_____   _____

_____   _____

_____   _____

_____   _____

_____   _____

_____   _____

LaVergne, TN USA
19 February 2010
173625LV00005B/1/P